D1525658

MURDER OFF THE RACK:

Critical Studies of Ten Paperback Masters

edited by
JON L. BREEN
and
MARTIN HARRY GREENBERG

The Scarecrow Press, Inc.
Metuchen, N.J., & London
1989

British Library Cataloguing-in-Publication data available

Library of Congress Cataloging-in-Publication Data

Murder off the rack : critical studies of ten paperback masters / edited by Jon L. Breen and Martin Harry Greenberg.
   p.   cm.
   Includes index.
   Contents: Introduction / by Jon L. Breen -- Harry Whittington / by Bill Crider -- Ed Lacy / by Marvin Lachman -- Jim Thompson / by Max Allan Collins -- The novels of Vin Packer / by Jon L. Breen -- Marvin H. Albert / by George Kelley -- Fifteen impressions of Charles Williams / by Ed Gorman -- Donald Hamilton / by Loren D. Estleman -- Peter Rabe / by Donald E. Westlake -- The executioner phenomenon / by Will Murray -- Warren Murphy and his heroic oddballs / by Dick Lochte.
   ISBN 0-8108-2232-6
   1. Detective and mystery stories, American -- History and criticism. 2. American fiction -- 20th century -- History and criticism. 3. Paperbacks -- United States.   I. Breen, Jon L., 1943- . II. Greenberg, Martin Harry.
PS374.D4M87 1989
813'.087209--dc20   89-33085

Manufactured in the United States of America

Printed on acid-free paper

ACKNOWLEDGMENTS

"Harry Whittington," copyright 1989 by Bill Crider.

"Ed Lacy: Paperback Writer of the Left," copyright 1989 by Marvin Lachman. (The author wishes to acknowledge the assistance of Don Cole, Edward D. Hoch, Bill Pronzini, and Charles Shibuk.)

"Jim Thompson: The Killers Inside Him," copyright 1989 by Max Allan Collins. (An earlier version of this essay appeared in *Jim Thompson: The Killers Inside Him*, Cedar Rapids, IA: Fedora Press, 1983.)

"The Novels of Vin Packer," copyright 1989 by Jon L. Breen.

"Marvin H. Albert," copyright 1989 by George Kelley.

"Fifteen Impressions of Charles Williams," copyright 1989 by Ed Gorman.

"Donald Hamilton: The Writing Crew," copyright 1989 by Loren D. Estleman.

"Peter Rabe," copyright 1989 by Donald E. Westlake.

"The Executioner Phenomenon," copyright 1989 by Will Murray.

"Warren Murphy and His Heroic Oddballs," copyright 1989 by Dick Lochte.

iii

TABLE OF CONTENTS

INTRODUCTION

Though there are scattered examples of paperback original mystery novels published in the thirties and the forties, the paperback crime novel is largely a product of the fifties and after. As the pulp magazines died, paperback originals came to take their place as a proving ground for new writers as well as a steady source of audience and income for a number of prolific professionals.

The first paperback originals, like most of the pulps, were geared to a male audience. The titles, along with the cover designs and blurbs, emphasized the lurid and the sexy, promised fast, violent action and hardboiled characters. The bestselling success of Mickey Spillane in the late forties helped to set much of the agenda. Though Spillane almost always appeared in hard covers first, his phenomenal sales were a big commercial factor in the fifties paperback industry. Not many of the paperback originals offered sex and violence as unfettered as Spillane's, but their blurbs were written as if they did.

Paperbacks were such a good deal for professional writers that some turned to them by choice though already well established in hardback--writers like Sax Rohmer, Bruno Fischer, and Wade Miller. Even such major figures in suspense fiction as Charlotte Armstrong and Cornell Woolrich made occasional appearances in original paperback. Ellery Queen and Brett Halliday both became paperback bylines, although most of the originals that appeared under those names were in fact ghost-written.

Paperbacks offered a larger advance, a larger sale, and more money sooner. In a typical reprint deal, the author would have to share the lucrative paperback earnings with the hardcover publisher. If the book went immediately into paperback, there was no need to share. Also, paperback publishers, with strict publication schedules to meet, had to make faster decisions than their hardcover counterparts. Thus, the author made more and made it faster. But there was a tradeoff to be made. Paperback originals were rarely reviewed, and paperback books then as now were often treated as disposable goods. Hardcovers did get reviewed; they got into libraries; they had permanence and snob appeal.

One wonders how much the paperback publishers owed to the one critic of the fifties who did consistently review paperback novels: Anthony Boucher of the *New York Times Book Review*. If there had not been the promise of a review from Boucher, would more of the highly talented paperback writers have fled to hard covers in the hope of some recognition?

Many writers made major contributions to the paperback original, and the present volume treats of only ten. How have these subjects been chosen? To a great degree by the special interests and preferences of the editors and contributors, but the following guidelines apply:

1) Each is known primarily as a paperback writer. All have at least occasionally been published in hardcover, but all have either made their greatest impact in paperback or have had the vast majority of their books published in that format. Jim Thompson started in the hardcover mainstream before finding his criminous softcover niche. Ed Lacy debuted as a mainstream hardcover novelist under another name and won an Edgar award for one of his hardcover novels,

but most of his novels appeared first in paper. Donald Hamilton published hardcover mysteries before becoming a softcover specialist. Don Pendleton, Warren Murphy, Marvin Albert, Charles Williams, and Vin Packer moved to hard covers only after years as paperback specialists. Only Peter Rabe and Harry Whittington were paperback writers first, last, and always, with hardback appearances rare aberrations.

2) All are representative of the tough, hard-boiled novel that typified the paperback original of the fifties. With the exception of Vin Packer (a pseudonym of ambiguous gender), all are male. All but two debuted in the fifties, and the two exceptions, Don Pendleton and Warren Murphy, are very much in the same tradition, in a direct line of descent from the dime novels and pulp magazines. In later decades, other types of mysteries--romantic suspense and classical puzzles--came to be published in paperback form, but those are matter for another book.

3) None of the subjects have received book-length critical attention. John D. MacDonald and Chester Himes were two of the most important authors of paperback originals in the fifties, but neither has been included here because both have had full-length critical studies devoted to their work. Of the writers included here, Jim Thompson has been the most extensively written about, but even he has not yet been the subject of a book-length study. Both Pendleton and Murphy have been the subject of fan-oriented secondary sources, but these can hardly be called critical.

Obviously, there are other notable writers who could have been covered in this book, enough to make up at least two additional volumes of comparable size. A few of them are Richard S. Prather, Jack Ehrlich, E. Howard Hunt (under various pseudonyms), Richard Deming, Wenzell Brown, Gil Brewer, Philip Atlee, Don

Von Elsner, James McKimmey, John McPartland, Frank Kane, Henry Kane, Harold R. Daniels, Norman Daniels, Stephen Marlowe, Day Keene, Michael Avallone, Jonathan Craig, Edward S. Aarons, Michael Brett, Dan J. Marlowe, Robert Colby, Richard Wormser, Carter Brown, and Lionel White.

The matter of style in the essays that follow has largely been left to the individual writers. In each case, the editors have appended a checklist to the end of the essay listing only those books referred to in the text, with U.S. publisher and date. For a full list of the author's works, the reader is referred to Allen J. Hubin's *Crime Fiction, 1749-1980: A Comprehensive Bibliography* (Garland, 1984) and its 1988 supplement, and John Reilly's *Twentieth Century Crime and Mystery Writers* (second edition, St. Martin's, 1985).

--Jon L. Breen

HARRY WHITTINGTON

by Bill Crider

Obsessed characters wracked by their passions--lust, greed, the desire for revenge--travel through the night-world of cheap bars, back-alley dives, and backwoods swamps: crooked cops and honorable ones, bent private eyes and those who live by a strict moral code, the dishonest and the noble, the seeking and the lost. Harry Whittington has written about them all, and many more, in a career that has covered parts of five decades. Under his own name and as Whit Harrison, Hallam Whitney, Harry White, Kell Holland, Clay Stuart, Harriet Kathryn Myers, and Ashley Carter, to name just a few, Whittington has been almost the prototypical paperback writer, always delivering a solid story and breakneck pacing for the reader's money. He has written, in addition to his mystery and suspense novels, Westerns, historical romances, backwoods romances, "mainstream" fiction, love stories, and nearly anything else that can be read, with the exception of science fiction and fantasy. He has written for such now-forgotten paperback houses as Handi-books, Uni, Phantom, Carnival, Venus, Original Novels, and Graphic, as well as for such famous houses as Fawcett Gold Medal, Avon, Pyramid, and Ace.

Whittington was particularly suited to the emerging paperback market of the early 1950s because of his ability to produce saleable fiction at a rapid pace. After the sale of his first softcover original, *Slay Ride for a Lady*, to James Quinn's Handi-Books in 1950, he wrote and sold twenty-five paperback originals in the next three years. Whittington tells about these years in an interview with Michael S. Barson in Billy

Lee's *Paperback Quarterly* (Volume 4, Number 2), explaining that "Gold Medal was the prestige paperback line" and that they also paid the best advance ($2500), while allowing writers to keep all foreign and movie rights. Gold Medal, after buying *Fires that Destroy* in 1951, naturally got to see most of Whittington's books before other publishers, and as Ashley Carter he continues to write for Gold Medal today, thirty-six years later, continuing the popular Blackoaks series. Other publishers in the early 1950s did not pay as well as Gold Medal, and Whittington recalls receiving a $750 advance for each of his Handi-books novels, while Ace paid him $1000 each for *Drawn to Evil* (1952) and *So Dead My Love!* (1953). He had a unique arrangement with Mauri Latzen, whose firm owned Carnival, Venus, Phantom, and Original Novels. He could submit a three-page outline at any time and receive a check for $375. After sending in the completed novel, he received another $375, and each reprinting brought an additional $375. Graphic, like Ace, paid a $1000 advance.

Considering the size of the advances, a writer had to produce a large number of books if he intended to make a living at his typewriter, particularly if, like Whittington, he had a growing family to support. In a 1978 address to the Florida Suncoast Writers' Conference (portions of which are reprinted in *Paperback Quarterly*, Volume 2, Number 2), Whittington says that he "chose consciously to write swiftly and with spontaneity" and that he "sold as fast as [he] could write." He was trying to make a living, and he did not have time to spend six months waiting for the prestigious hardback houses to make a decision about his work. He needed to sell, and he needed the quick decisions of the paperback market, despite its lack of prestige. After all, hardcover snob appeal is not everything, and when reviewers did begin to notice paperback originals, Whittington received excellent notices. Anthony Boucher, surely one of the shrewdest critics the field of mystery and suspense has ever known, was one of the first to devote regular space to paperback authors, and in his "Criminals at Large" column in *The New York Times Book Review* he called Whittington "one of the most versatile and satisfactory creators" of the paperback original. In a review of *You'll Die Next!* (Ace, 1954), Boucher wrote that Whittington was capable of "the best sheer story-telling since the greatest days of the pre-sex detective pulps."

Such comments were the result of Whittington's ability to produce books that combined fast action, clever plotting, and three-dimensional characters in a rapidly-paced story. In his article "The Paperback Original," published in *The Mystery Writer's Handbook* (ed. Herbert Brean, Harper, 1956), Whittington writes, "it's as true in paperbacks as in trade editions--maybe even truer--that you must tell a vital, hard-hitting story; you've got to keep it moving and give it that old emotional pull." This was a lesson that Whittington had learned well, but there is more. The writer must also "Care. Make the characters come alive; get so involved in those people you're writing about that you yourself want to race right along beside them and see that they come out all right." All Whittington's best work involves characters the reader cares about, in situations which at first seem simple. The characters have goals that seem easily obtainable, but unexpected complications arise. Things suddenly get worse, and then worse still. Finally, when the character seems doomed or hopelessly trapped, when it appears that things could not possibly get any worse, they do. A good example of this technique is found in Whittington's first paperback, *Slay Ride for a Lady* (Handi-books, 1950). Narrator, Dan Henderson, an ex-cop framed for murder, is released from prison to find the wife of a criminal/political bigshot. He finds the woman almost at once, but then she is killed. Henderson is framed again, beaten to a pulp by vicious cops, and betrayed by a girl he trusts. He survives, even prevails, but there is no false happy ending such as some writers might provide. It just wouldn't work in a story this hard-boiled, and though Whittington does believe in a happy ending most of the time, he avoids it here. In addition to refusing to provide the expected upbeat conclusion, Whittington throws in another unique touch. The murdered woman has a baby for whom Henderson feels a sense of responsibility. There is a memorable episode in which Henderson, chasing a murderer, blood pouring down his arm from a knife wound in his shoulder, pauses to feed the baby its milk from a bottle. Has any other hard-boiled hero ever done the same?

The device of the man framed for murder was one to which Whittington returned often and effectively, especially in two of his novels for Graphic, *Call Me Killer* (1951) and *Mourn the Hangman* (1952). The former combines the murder frame with amnesia as Sam Gowan, soft-boiled nebbish who is a far cry from Dan Henderson, wakes up in the office of a prominent businessman who has very recently been shot in the face. Sam is holding a gun and certainly appears to be a likely suspect in the murder. His situation is further complicated by the fact that he has been missing from home for some months and, as the reader eventually learns, has constructed for himself an alternate identity as "David Mye" while suffering from a loss of memory. Add to this a brutal cop named Barney Manton, who is determined to crack the case and pin the murder on Sam, no matter how illegally he has to proceed, and the result is a typical fast-paced Whittington story. In *Mourn the Hangman*, Steve Blake, a private eye working on a case involving a government supplier who is cheating on his contracts, is framed for the murder of his wife. He is pursued by the police, hunted by the bad guys, betrayed by his partner, and put through more twists and turns of plot than would seem

possible. Like Sam Gowan, he hardly has time even to
eat or sleep as he tries to set things right.

Gowan and Blake are typical Whittington
protagonists, but he was anything but formula bound,
as a look at another of his Graphic novels, *Murder is
My Mistress* (1951), demonstrates. The title is entirely
misleading--there is no murder in the novel. That
fact alone is enough to make the book different from
the typical mystery paperback. And, murder is no
one's mistress. In fact, the book's main character is a
woman, and the story is one of psychological suspense
as it follows the life of Julia Clarkson, whose past
catches up with her. Now a middle-class housewife,
Julia had twenty years earlier been the companion of a
criminal, Paul Renner. She informed on him to escape
the life she was living, but now she learns that he has
been released from prison and begins to fear for her
life. He torments her with a series of "accidents," and
her life and marriage deteriorate rapidly.

Another female protagonist, though a very
different one, is Bernice Harper, the mousy secretary
of *Fires that Destroy* (Gold Medal, 1951). Bernice kills
and robs her employer, a wealthy blind man, and gets
away with it. Well, almost. Whittington's killers
never *quite* get away with murder, though they often
come close. The punishments that Whittington sets up
for them are always interesting and always grow out of
their characters. The punishments are also always
wonderfully ironic, as in the case of Bernice and
especially in the case of the lawyer in the excellent
Web of Murder (Gold Medal, 1958), one of
Whittington's best and most cleverly-plotted novels.
The lawyer and his secretary, with whom he is having
an affair, decide to kill the lawyer's wife. They
succeed, but they are confronted with a cop much like
Barney Manton from *Call Me Killer* (though this time
the cop is an honest one). He is convinced that the
pair are guilty of murder, but can he prove it? It

would not be fair to tell, but it is not revealing too
much to say that things--lots of little things--do
begin to go wrong with the lawyer's beautifully
planned "perfect" murder, leading to one plot surprise
after another. Though each twist is carefully
prepared for, each works to perfection, right up to the
powerhouse conclusion.

A similar story, but one which does not work
quite as well, is *The Humming Box* (Ace, 1956). The
female protagonist, Liz Palmer, discovers a unique
murder method and uses it to rid herself of the
husband she no longer cares for, and of course to get
his money. While not as strong a story as *Web of
Murder*, this novel nevertheless has its moments, as Liz
succeeds with murder only to be preyed on by a very
slimy private detective before she meets her ironic
fate.

Lethal women, though they figure prominently in
Whittington's work, are not always the protagonists.
Often they are secondary to the men who fall--and
fall hard--for them. In *Satan's Widow* (Phantom,
1951), tough cop Barney Hodges falls for the widow of
"Satan," a terrible but powerful man who, when alive,
delighted in ruining people's lives. When Satan is
poisoned, Hodges is certain the wife is guilty, though
there are plenty of other suspects. He is so
powerfully attracted to her, however, that he is
determined to see that she is not arrested, no matter
who he has to frame for the crime. Her guilt or
innocence becomes irrelevant to him. There is a
definite James M. Cain influence on this novel, and the
sex scenes are fairly steamy stuff for a 1951 mass
market book. In *The Mystery Writer's Handbook*,
Whittington says that *Satan's Widow* is a revised
version of a serial, *Body in the Bedroom*, that he
wrote for the King Features Syndicate. He sold the
novel against his agent's and editor's better judgment,
but it was reprinted in five foreign countries and

earned its author a lot of money, "although everybody
says it stinks." Whittington evidently liked the novel
well enough to use a *very* similar plot in a much
stronger book, *Drawn to Evil* (Ace, 1952), in which the
tough cop, once more drawn irresistibly to the prime
suspect--the dead man's wife--goes so far as to
conceal evidence and frame another, less likely, suspect
for the crime. How tough is this cop? Listen:

> I let him make his play. Before he got his
> knife out, I had a wad of shirt front in my fist.
> I jerked him off balance. When he spread his
> legs to steady himself, I drove my knee into his
> groin. Hard.
>
> I released him without even looking at him
> again. I heard something clatter on the floor.
> It must have been his long-bladed slap-knife.
> He wasn't going to need it for a while. Not
> while he writhed.

Despite the similarity of this novel to *Satan's Widow*,
they are two distinct stories, with completely
different ways of working out the various plot threads.
Overall, *Drawn to Evil* is the more successful and
satisfactory book, and it has a bang-up ending that
can stand with the best of Whittington's work.

Another novel with a dangerously attractive
woman is *A Night for Screaming* (Ace, 1960), which
also brings in a framed man on the run. Mitch
Walker is a former cop innocent of the murder of
which he is accused, though naturally he can't prove
it. He is pursued by his brutal former partner, Fred
Palmer, and winds up on a wheat farm in Kansas.
(How many suspense novels set on wheat farms can
you name? Leave it to Harry Whittington to come up
with a setting like this and to make it seem absolutely
real.) The farm is owned by Mr. Barton M. Cassel and

looks like a good place to hide from the law, except
that the work is brutal, the pay is low, and when Mr.
Cassel's wife, Eve, takes a liking to you, well, sixteen
hours in the sun at manual labor might be easier.
There are plenty of twists in the story, and the
suspense, a Whittington hallmark, never lets up.

The man-on-the-run theme also figures
prominently in *You'll Die Next!* (Ace, 1954), in which
Henry Wilson, an ordinary guy married to a woman
whose past he knows little about, is viciously beaten,
receives a threatening letter, loses his job, is involved
in a hit-and-run accident (as the victim), and is
accused both of beating his wife and shooting a cop--
all in the first fifty pages. In the *New York Times
Book Review*, Anthony Boucher wrote, "*You'll Die Next!*
is a very short novel, which is just as well. I
couldn't have held my breath any longer in this
vigorous tale whose plot is too dexterously twisted
even to mention in a review." High praise indeed,
especially coming from Boucher, but certainly justified
in the case of one of Whittington's cleverest stories.

Whittington also dealt effectively with the theme
of "one man against municipal corruption." A prime
example is found in *Violent Night* (under the name
Whit Harrison, Phantom, 1951). Coast Town is a
hotbed of teen prostitutes, dope dealers, and gambling
dens. O'Brian, an honest cop with an invalid wife,
has to deal with his mistress' leaving him, suspension
from the police force, a hired killer imported into
town to murder him, and a dead teenage girl found
beside the road with three poker chips in her shoe.
No one but Whittington could deal successfully with so
many plot threads in such a short (128 pages) book,
while compressing all the events into the period of a
single fast-moving night. He succeeds almost as well
in *So Dead My Love!* (Ace, 1953). Jim Talbot, a New
York private eye, is called home to Duval, Florida, by
the man who got his conviction overturned and got

him out of one of Florida's toughest prisons some
years before. The man is now married to Talbot's
former sweetheart, the very woman who got him into
prison in the first place. It's Talbot's job to locate a
missing man, and in doing so he must deal with a fat,
nasty sheriff who likes things just as they are and his
psychopathic deputy. The small-town southern setting
adds spice to the plot.

In fact, Whittington is particularly good at
depicting the small towns and rural areas of 1950s
Florida, and readers should not overlook certain of
his books simply because their titles do not suggest
mysteries. For example, *Backwoods Tramp* (Gold
Medal, 1959) might seem from its title and cover to be
a sort of "cracker romance" along the lines of
Backwoods Shack or *Backwoods Hussy* (both of which
first appeared under the Hallam Whitney name), but it
is instead a powerful suspense story. It does feature
an archetypal southern poor-white woman as a love
interest, but it is really the story of Jake Richards,
who is searching the swamp country for Marve Pooser,
the man who engineered the robbery that cost Jake his
job, his girl, and his reputation. Pooser is a
psychopath any reader can hate, and Richards is a
believable protagonist, no hero but a man who learns
quite a bit about himself and his motives. By the end
of the novel, Richards is able to face what he has
become in his search for Pooser and to avoid becoming
something worse.

A man who faces what he has become and doesn't
even seem to care is the crooked cop Mike Ballard in
Brute in Brass (Gold Medal, 1956). Ballard is at first a
completely contemptible man, callous, indifferent to
others, concerned only with himself and what he can
get, no matter how he gets it. He always looks for
the angle, the way to turn any situation to his own
advantage. Little by little, Whittington reveals the
reasons for Ballard's attitudes and surprises the reader

by eventually eliciting sympathy for the man. Despite the book's strengths as a character study, however, it moves at the typical jet-like pace of any Whittington novel, a neat trick but one that Whittington pulled off with regularity.

Two more books that should not escape anyone's notice are *Married to Murder* (Phantom, 1951) and *Body and Passion* (as Whit Harrison, Original Novels, 1952). The former is the story of yet another cop framed for murder, one of Whittington's seemingly infinite and original variations on a single plot idea. The cop, Palmer, agrees to undergo plastic surgery and pose as the son-in-law of a wealthy New York woman in order to travel to Florida and help the woman's daughter, who is in some unspecified kind of trouble. Before he quite knows what is happening, he has had his appearance altered and finds himself sitting in the front seat of a car with a dead body in his lap, a body the old woman has been keeping in her freezer and whose dead face bears a striking and unsettling resemblance to the face Palmer now sees when he looks into the mirror. To top it off, when he gets to Florida, Palmer finds the daughter being kept as a virtual prisoner in her own house, held there in a drug-induced haze by none other than Palmer's larcenous and treacherous ex-wife.

Palmer's identity crisis, however, can't hold a candle to the problems of the protagonist of *Body and Passion*. He doesn't know who he is, and neither does anyone else. Two men, one a gangster and one an ambitious assistant district attorney, are trapped in a terrible fire at the gangster's hideaway cabin. Only one man survives, and he is so badly burned that there is no way to recognize him or even to take his fingerprints. (On the book's cover he is depicted as what cover-art critic Art Scott has called "the mummy in the tuxedo.") The D.A.'s parents want him to be their precious son, the mob wants to kill him, and the girl who loved the gangster wants him to marry her. But he simply can't remember his identity, despite living for a week both as D.A. and as gangster. And if that isn't enough, it turns out that a third man, a newspaper reporter who was spying on both the other men, has also disappeared on the night of the fire. The protagonist, X as he is called throughout most of the story, does recover his memory, but Whittington manages to keep the reader guessing most of the way through this unusual suspense novel.

Because he has written over one hundred paperback novels, Whittington did not manage to come up with a winner every single time, which is not surprising considering the amount of work. After all, even Sandy Koufax lost a few ball games. Two books that don't quite live up to the author's usual high standards are *One Got Away* (Ace, 1955) and *Hot as Fire--Cold as Ice* (Belmont, 1962). In *One Got Away*, a man named Gosucki steals plans worth one million dollars from the government. Dan Campbell, who was assigned to watch Gosucki, tries to redeem himself by catching the thief, and in doing so travels from Chicago to Carolina to Indianapolis to Hawaii, while being pursued by his own agency. The chase elements and the race against time don't quite click in this one. *Hot as Fire* fails for different reasons, as a deep-freeze salesman tries to foil kidnappers who are keeping a dead body in a freezer he has sold them. It's a thin plot, a far cry from the incident-packed twists and turns of Whittington's best work.

According to Mike Barson's introduction to the interview for *Paperback Quarterly*, Whittington "retired from the paperback field in disgust" from 1969 to 1975, "convinced he was demeaning himself" after writing a series of movie and television show "novelizations," Westerns, and nurse novels for little pay and even less prestige. One of these novels was, however, one of Whittington's biggest successes with readers if not in a financial sense. Whittington, who also did many of the lead novels for *The Man from U.N.C.L.E.* magazine, wrote *The Doomsday Affair* (*The Man from U.N.C.L.E. #2*) for Ace books. The book proved to be extremely popular with fans of the television series and drew more mail than any of Whittington's previous works. The book apparently sold well, but the sale did not particularly benefit the author, series books of this sort usually being on a work-for-hire basis and paying a flat fee instead of a royalty.

In 1975, Whittington began his comeback in the paperback field. As Ashley Carter, he took over Gold Medal's Falconhurst and Blackoaks series of slave/plantation historical novels and once more found himself a best-selling writer. Since that time he has written other historical works (*Panama*, Gold Medal, 1978), mainstream novels (*Rampage*, Gold Medal, 1978), and Westerns (six novels in Jove's Longarm series). Most of these books, though longer by far than the lean, mean novels Whittington wrote in the 1950s, nevertheless retain most of the virtues of the earlier works--clever plotting, fast pacing, and expert story-telling.

In spite of his well-deserved successes in the past twelve years, it is for his earlier work that readers of mystery and suspense fiction will remember Harry Whittington. He has said that his favorite writers at that time were Frederick C. Davis, Day Keene, and Fredric Brown, and that if there was any influence on his work it was James M. Cain. Readers might also note the influence of Cornell Woolrich, and Whittington encouraged would-be paperback writers to read Fitzgerald, Faulkner, Hemingway, Dostoyevski, O'Hara, and Wouk in his article in *The Mystery Writer's Handbook*. He also mentioned Brown, Woolrich, Chandler, and Roy Huggins. Some of these writers are revered today, some forgotten; some are still in print, others not. For far too long Whittington's has been the latter case, his best works available only to those willing to spend long hours in dusty used-book stores, searching through stacks of crumbling paperbacks in the hopes, in the hopes . . . . An enterprising publisher, Black Lizard Books, has done something to remedy this situation by bringing back into print a number of Whittington's mystery and suspense novels. The readers who buy these books will have a lot of pleasure in store, presented to them by a master of the suspense novel, who will provide them with a gallery of believable characters in incredibly tense situations, pushed to the extremes of their mental and physical abilities, plunged into despair but never quite losing hope, always struggling, always alive. Of the great paperback writers of the 1950s, Jim Thompson eventually attracted a cult following. John D. MacDonald went on to take his place on the hardcover best-seller lists. Harry Whittington, on the other hand, saw his best work fall into neglect. Let us hope that posterity will rediscover his books and recognize him as what he is: one of the true masters of paperback fiction.

Checklist: Harry Whittington

Backwoods Hussy (as Hallam Whitney) (Paperback Library, 1952)
Backwoods Shack (as Hallam Whitney) (Paperback Library, 1954)
Backwoods Tramp (Gold Medal, 1959)
Body and Passion (as Whit Harrison) (Original Novels, 1952)
Brute in Brass (Gold Medal, 1956)
Call Me Killer (Graphic, 1951)
The Doomsday Affair (Ace, 1965)
Drawn to Evil (Ace, 1952)
Fires that Destroy (Gold Medal, 1951)
Hot as Fire--Cold as Ice (Belmont, 1962)

The Humming Box (Ace, 1956)
Married to Murder (Phantom, 1951)
Mourn the Hangman (Graphic, 1952)
Murder Is My Mistress (Graphic, 1951)
A Night for Screaming (Ace, 1960)
One Got Away (Ace, 1955)
Panama (as Ashley Carter) (Gold Medal, 1978)
Rampage (Gold Medal, 1978)
Satan's Widow (Phantom, 1951)
Slay Ride for a Lady (Handi-Books, 1950)
So Dead My Love! (Ace, 1953)
Violent Night (as Whit Harrison) (Phantom, 1951)
You'll Die Next! (Ace, 1954)
Web of Murder (Gold Medal, 1958)

ED LACY: PAPERBACK WRITER OF THE LEFT

by Marvin Lachman

The mystery has usually been the province of writers with right-wing viewpoints. English mysteries between the World Wars created a climate Colin Watson described as "snobbery with violence." The thrillers of Sydney Horler and H. C. McNeile often had Jews, Italians, and others who were not Anglo-Saxon as villains. Even Agatha Christie, though less obvious, included gratuitous anti-Semitic remarks. In the United States, writers like Cleve F. Adams, Mickey Spillane, Richard S. Prather, E. Howard Hunt, William F. Buckley, and Elizabeth Linington delivered political messages favoring the right. Ed Lacy was virtually the only American mystery writer consistently to espouse the causes of underdogs, and his opinions were generally those of the political left. He was not above delivering polemics, and these occasionally detracted from his mysteries. Yet his willingness to expand the boundaries of the mystery, by writing of people who had suffered discrimination, made Lacy one of the most interesting writers of paperback originals.

"Ed Lacy" was one of two pseudonyms used by Len Zinberg for his mysteries; the other, used in short stories, was "Steve April." Before he began writing mysteries, Zinberg, who was born in New York City in 1911, wrote short stories for magazines like *Coronet*, *The New Yorker*, *Collier's*, and *Esquire*. He also published a novel about boxing, *Walk Hard--Talk Loud* in 1940. It was adapted for the Broadway stage in 1944, with former middleweight champion Mickey Walker making his acting debut. During World War II, Zinberg was a correspondent for *Yank*. When he returned he wrote two more mainstream novels, *What D'ya Know for Sure* (1947), winner of a Twentieth Century Fox-Doubleday Award, and *Hold with the Hares* (1948), before launching his career as a writer of mysteries, mainly original paperbacks. As Lacy he won the Mystery Writers of America (MWA) Best Novel Edgar for *Room to Swing* (1957). Zinberg died in New York City of a heart attack on January 7, 1968, leaving a wife, Esther, and daughter, Carla.

In *The Third Degree*, the official publication of MWA, for January 1968, D. R. Bensen wrote:

> Ed was a big, bearish man, who spoke in a kind of baritone growl; roughly dressed, most times I saw him as if he had just come from a stint of duty as a truck dispatcher--unslick, definitely. He was also unfailingly good-humored in a wry way, perceptive, and kind; and was one of the very best writers going when it came to conveying moods of tension and fast action, and convincing the reader that it was a believable human being, not a puppet, who was experiencing what he described. We will miss his presence and the work he would have done very much.

Lacy had two separate careers in paperback originals, writing five novels from 1951 to 1954 before publishing the first of five hardcover mysteries for Harper and Row between 1955 and 1958. The hardcovers brought him outstanding reviews and his Edgar. Yet, after 1958 his mysteries were no longer published in hardcover, and attempts to learn why from various sources, including his former editor, Joan Kahn, proved fruitless. Of course, Lacy cannot give his version, and it is difficult to find the executor of his literary estate, as Matthew J. Bruccoli learned in 1986 when he tried to obtain reprint rights to a short story for *New Black Mask*. Since Lacy's last hardcover novel, *Be Careful How You Live* (1958), was one of

his weaker books, one can assume that if subsequent
mysteries were turned down, Lacy went back to a more
certain market, paperback originals. He remained
prolific, publishing eighteen paperback novels in about
twelve years. He also contributed extensively to
digest-sized mystery magazines, eventually publishing at
least one hundred short stories, mostly between 1958
and 1969, in *Manhunt*, *Ellery Queen's Mystery Magazine*
and almost every other market available.

Bigotry and its manifestations is the most
important theme running through Lacy's work. As a
white man who was married to a black woman, Zinberg
was especially conscious of this. Not only are blacks
frequently and fairly portrayed, but so are others
against whom there has traditionally been
discrimination, e.g., women, Jews, Puerto Ricans,
Italians, Greeks, and American Indians. Lacy was
ahead of his time in using a black private detective,
Toussaint Marcus Moore of *Room to Swing*, as a hero.
Perhaps Hollywood was not yet ready in the late
1950s, before the civil rights movement had reached
full flower, for a black detective in films. Certainly,
Lacy's entire career might have been different had a
movie about Moore been made that was as good as *In
the Heat of the Night*, using John Ball's Virgil Tibbs, a
decade later. Lacy's use of blacks (they were still
called Negroes then) began with his second novel, *Sin
in Their Blood* (1952), in which blacks passing as white
are blackmailed by a right-wing organization. A
dignified Negro maid is treated with disrespect by the
local police but with courtesy by the book's hero,
private eye Matt Ranzino, who was thrown off the
force when he arrested the mayor's cousin for drunk
driving. (Police brutality and corruption were
frequently used by Lacy until he, himself, created
policemen as series characters.)

In *Go for the Body* (1954), Lacy's last paperback
before his hardcover phase, he created a major black

protagonist, "Bud" Stewart, an American boxer married
to a French woman. He remained in France after
World War II because of racial prejudice, saying, "I'm
only staying here because in France I can be an
American. In America I can only be a Negro . . . .
I'm *monsieur* over here. In the states a Negro is 'boy'
until he's 70, then he becomes 'uncle,' but never
mister" (pages 64, 77).

After Toussaint "Touie" Moore's award-winning
appearance in hardcover, Lacy used him only once
again, in a paperback original, *Moment of Untruth*
(1964). In both books Lacy successfully put the
reader into the mind of a black man. In *Room to
Swing*, Moore is on a case in southern Ohio, an area
which at the time closely mirrored the deep South in
racial attitudes. In his second book, he is in Mexico.
While he finds less overt discrimination, he sees subtle
prejudice. A promiscuous white woman assumes that
all black males, including Moore, want to have sex
with her until happily married Moore sets her straight.
The book contains subtly written conversations between
Moore and another black whom he meets after arriving.
Moore asks him, "How's things here?" (page 30). It is
immediately clear he is asking how blacks are treated
in Mexico City.

Lacy's second series character, Dave Wintino,
who also appeared first in hardcover, in *Lead with
Your Left* (1957), has a black partner named Danny
Hayes. Defending his absent partner against racial
slurs, Wintino slugs another policeman. Hayes is
philosophical when he hears of the incident, telling
Wintino, ". . . sometimes people say things without
meaning real harm. Just been raised ignorantly . . .
you can't take on the world" (page 40). But Dave's
attitude is "I'll never eat crow for any bigoted
knucklehead who makes cracks about my race or
religion" (page 41). Wintino must overcome his
youthful appearance (he is the youngest detective on

the New York City Police Department) but also prejudice because of his Italian-Jewish background. Wintino's last appearance was in *Double Trouble* (1965). Still plagued by his "baby face," Wintino is now the youngest NYPD lieutenant but has trouble convincing people that he is not just a kid.

Lee Hayes was the more militant black policeman Lacy created as his third and last series character. The two Hayes books, *Harlem Underground* (1965) and *In Black and Whitey* (1967), both original paperbacks, are set during the racial riots of the 1960s and in both Hayes' assignments are based on color. In the first book Hayes' youthful appearance permits him to infiltrate a teen-age black gang which, manipulated by a man called "Purple Eyes," is bent on creating chaos and bringing New York to a halt. Both Hayes books contain frequent debates with a veteran black police lieutenant regarding the best means to overcome past racial prejudice and whether violence is ever justified. Hayes believes in upholding law and order, but he is not sanguine that anything short of bloodshed can redress past grievances.

There were times when Lacy allowed his feelings to interfere with his storytelling gifts as he included scenes and dialogue which, while demonstrating discrimination, interrupted his mystery plot. One example is Wintino's fight. In the same book, Rose Hondura, a Puerto Rican nationalist, refers to her land as "a colony," but it has nothing to do with the story. Jose, the 14-year-old hero of Lacy's young adult mystery, *Sleep in Thunder* (1964), is introduced in terms of the discrimination he and his family, as Puerto Ricans, have received. Yet, as Lacy's story unfolds, events seem to belie this, since Jose is treated well, especially by the police. In the short novel, "Coin of Adventure," included in *Two Hot to Handle* (1963), a character claims that Willie Mays is not a good baseball player because he is black. Lacy, not

too subtly, in the denouement makes this bigot into a
neo-Nazi.   Lacy   constantly   criticizes   capitalism,
especially the advertising business.   ("Gray flannel" is
used almost as an epithet.) In *Breathe No More, My
Lady* (1958), a young advertising copywriter is
manipulated so that his career depends on the decision
whether to reissue books by a writer accused of
murder.   Other   elements   of   the   "establishment,"
including business, the police, and the government, are
invariably   portrayed   as   corrupt.   Rosa   Hondura   is
harassed by a large company because she plans to
write an article exposing their business practices.   A
self-employed printer in *The Napalm Bugle* (1968) is
subjected to U.S. government pressure because he
prints the small newspaper published by the pacifist
hero.   Whites often come off badly in Lacy.   A
moderate black in *In Black and Whitey* says, "Every
white has so damn much bigotry hidden within him"
(page 24).   In books set in the South Pacific, whites
are consistently ridiculed as inhibited regarding sex,
yet derided for their hypocrisy as bringers of venereal
disease to the natives.

Often, individual criminal acts are justified by
root causes such as discrimination, and detectives feel
guilty in apprehending perpetrators.   For example,
Touie Moore calls himself an "Uncle Tom" when he
regards a Mexican Indian as a murder suspect.   In
Lacy's first book, *The Woman Aroused* (1951), a leftist
feels guilt at having killed, albeit in self defense, a
poor Puerto Rican hired by politicians to murder him.
Italian leftists in "Coin of Adventure" are incredibly
brave and loyal compared to the cynical American
protagonist, who is apolitical.

The U.S. government is dangerously inefficient as
well as venal in *The Napalm Bugle*.   Lacy also inserts
a gratuitous scene of crime on the New York subway
in which he conveniently has three young hoodlums
who are white, black, and Latin harass his hero.

Showing that criminals are not limited to a single race, while true, adds nothing to the plot. In the same book, equating the U.S. bombing of Hiroshima to the Holocaust is unsubtle anti-Americanism.

Lacy was also ahead of his time regarding equality of the sexes. In *The Freeloaders* (1961), Doris, one of his successful businesswomen, is given to talking about "male jingoism," an early equivalent of the phrase "male chauvinism" which became so popular later. Grace Lupe-Varon, a college professor in *Moment of Truth*, is a feminist who alludes to God as "Her." Only in his treatment of homosexual males did Lacy reflect existing attitudes. They were referred to as "queers" or "faggots," with never any attempt to render fully rounded and/or sympathetic characters.

The sport of boxing recurs throughout Lacy. No mystery writer before or since has written more often or more knowledgeably about it. Lacy's interest in boxing long predated his career as a mystery writer. In addition to Zinberg's boxing novel, an earlier story, "For His Kids," in *Coronet* (October 1938), concerns a strange suburban boxing match between two fathers.

Although only two of Lacy's mysteries have boxing as a main theme, well over half contain boxing action or include characters who are former boxers. Lacy's boxing mysteries, *Go for the Body* and *The Big Fix* (1960), are among his best works. The former is practically a clinic on how the sport operates in Europe, especially how officials favor the local boxers. Lacy writes, ". . . whoring and pro boxing are alike-- both selling bodies. Ever see a rich guy go in for leather slinging? You don't because only one thing makes a guy take punishment for pay--he's poor, hungry-poor. Same for a girl who starts selling it, and that goes for the babes walking Eighth Avenue or Wabash Avenue or Sunset Boulevard" (page 83). *Sin in Their Blood*, the first mystery in which Lacy mentions boxing, includes an old friend of Ranzino, "Pops," who managed him when he was an amateur boxer. "Pops" talked Matt out of being a professional boxer, telling him, "man only becomes a fighter because he can't make pork chops any other way" (page 113).

Lead with Your Left sounds like the perfect title for a sports story, but has more to do with the politics of the leading characters than with boxing, though Dave Wintino, once an amateur boxer, K.O.s a bigot. The combination of boxing and politics continues in *Breathe No More, My Lady*, with a blacklisted left-wing professor who once had to earn a living as a professional boxer. He pictures the sport as one men will only take up out of desperation: ". . . it isn't glory that makes men fight, only hunger" (pages 50-51). Lacy apparently had a love-hate relationship with boxing. However, in his somewhat simplistic philosophy, he never considered that some people would choose to be boxers (or prostitutes) rather than accept the "grind" of a 9 a.m. to 5 p.m. job.

Throughout Lacy's work, there is reference to the great boxers of the past. In *Shakedown for Murder* (1958), a Long Island police chief is described as "looking like heavyweight Max Baer in his prime." Other comparisons in that book are to Rocky Marciano and Floyd Patterson. *The Big Fix* alludes to the boxers of the 1950s including "Sugar Ray" Robinson, Carmen Basilio, Billie Graham, Archie Moore, and Jake LaMotta. It also accurately describes how television almost destroyed boxing during the decade, putting small clubs out of business when they could not compete with the availability of free bouts.

The Big Fix is about little Tommy Cork, an average welterweight who once fought Robinson but now is relegated to insignificant four-rounders. He is separated from his wife only because they can no longer afford an apartment. In a poignant scene, which works surprisingly well, she begs him to take a job as a dishwasher (she is a waitress) so together they can save enough to buy furniture. Tommy is reluctant to give up boxing, especially when an apparent miracle appears in the form of Arno Brewer, a wealthy man who offers to stake Cork's comeback, claiming to be obsessed with the sport: "Some guys go for boxing as if it were dope" (page 19). However, Arno is also practical enough to insure Cork's life for $50,000. A friend of Cork's becomes suspicious and goes to police detective Walter Steiner, himself a former Olympic boxing champion. The investigation leads to a climax which is spellbinding. Even if *The Big Fix* is unlikely in its insurance scheme premise, it is one of Lacy's best books and would have made a fine film, one to fit into that small sub-genre, the boxing *film noir*, e.g., *Body and Soul*, *The Set-Up*, *Champion*, and *Killer McCoy*. *The Big Fix* could have had Mickey Rooney as Cork. (His performance as Killer McCoy, generally forgotten now, is probably his finest adult movie role.) Rod Steiger would have been an ideal Arno.

Even in his 1960s paperbacks, set in exotic locales like the Riviera and the South Pacific, Lacy invariably included one character who had been a boxer, and in at least seven of these books he has a confrontation between the ex-fighter and a judo or karate expert. The fighter always wins, usually by faking a right hand and delivering a quick left hand punch as knockout blow before the martial arts specialist can counter.

Lacy consistently made his heroes "different." He had black series characters when they were rare. Hal Darling in *Strip for Violence* (1953) has to overcome his diminutive stature (he is only 5' 1") and must fight people who think they can take advantage of his size. They can't, because Darling is adept at

both boxing and judo. Wintino has a baby face and is
defensive about it. Matt Ranzino has come home from
Korea with a lung removed due to tuberculosis. He's
afraid of physical exertion and drinks milk for his
health. In a scene which is almost a parody, Ranzino,
the former boxer, tries to avoid a fight with bullies
who taunt him about drinking milk, then call him a
"wop and a dago." Inevitably he is drawn back into
action to solve a murder.

Anthony Boucher praised *Bugged for Murder*
(1961) as "a good study of a man coming to terms
with an invalid body" (*New York Times Book Review*,
10 September, 1961). Billy Wallace, a private eye who
suffered a heart attack at age 38, is living a reclusive
life. He is afraid of sex and physical activity,
spending his days watching television. His wife and a
friend try rehabilitation by giving him a job which
appears only to involve electronic surveillance.
However, a murder occurs, and Billy is required to
perform the kind of physical activity which tests his
heart as well as his resolve. Yet, this does not happen
until after he backs away from a fight with a brutal,
taunting bartender who, coincidentally, he once sent to
prison. Brad Armstrong of *The Napalm Bugle* returned
from Korea with a Medal of Honor, a hook instead of
a right hand, and pacifist opinions.

If some of Lacy's women were liberated, the
most distinctive thing about most of them was their
physique. Of course, Lacy's women were "stacked";
that was par for the paperback course. However, Lacy
went a step further and wrote about women who can
only be described as Amazons. The first of Lacy's
large women, the amoral Lee, his titular heroine in *The
Woman Aroused*, was over six feet tall. In his very
last book, *The Big Bust* (1969), we read, "at 5' 11", 160
lbs. Rhoda was not only the largest woman on the
beach, but her shapely bigness was pure sensual
excitement" (page 7).

When his protagonists were not distinctive due
to race or physical characteristics, they were often set
apart by being artists or writers. Lacy used two
artists, and they were remarkably similar. Sculptor
Marshal Jameson begins *Enter Without Desire* (1954) as
narrator, telling the reader he is waiting to kill a man.
He is an ex-college football player from Kentucky, now
living in The Bronx (scene of many Lacy books). The
book unfortunately has a soap opera-ish plot about
jealousy and failed marriages. The story is no better
in *The Sex Castle* (1963), about Clayton Biner, another
ex-football player who is a failure in marriage and as
an abstract painter. He also narrates the book through
flashbacks, thus giving away more of the unlikely plot
than is necessary. Lacy has involved Biner, purely by
the accident of a passport mix-up, in an unbelievable
mystery about drug traffic.

Fortunately, the books about writers are far
better, except for *The Woman Aroused*, in which
George Jackson edits the house organ for an oil
company. Like most Lacy "heroes," he has an
unhappy marriage. In fact, he and Flo are divorced,
though periodically they try a reunion, which usually
ends in a fight and her calling him, as the ultimate
insult, "you . . . you writer" (page 8). The mystery
elements in this book are negligible, making it appear
that Lacy had started his paperback career as a writer
of sexy mainstream fiction.

A far better book involving a writer is *Breathe
No More, My Lady*, in which "Mad Matt" Anthony, an
Ernest Hemingway type, is accused of murder on Long
Island. While Norm Connor, who writes advertising
copy for Anthony's publisher, tries to prove him
innocent, "Mad Matt" cleverly writes a book about his
own trial, while it is taking place, saying at one point,
". . . and the condemned man wrote a hearty last
chapter" (page 168). Lacy has the prosecution use as

evidence an article that Anthony wrote for MWA's *The
Third Degree*, attempting to prove that he had
knowledge of murder methods. Since Anthony is a
mystery writer, it is not clear why this is useful,
especially since the article was about guns and the
victim died of a blow to the head. Since Lacy himself
was active in MWA, he may have intended an inside
joke when he worked the last name of Stanley Ellin
into two books, referring to the Ellin Detective Agency
in *Bugged for Murder* and inserting a teen-age baseball
player named Larry Ellin into *Sleep in Thunder*.

Lacy's last book, *The Big Bust*, also concerns a
Long Island writer of Hemingway-like eccentricities,
who hires a private eye, John O'Hara, to recover
$62,000 stolen from him. (O'Hara reminds people he is
not John O'Hara, the writer.) A third Long Island
writer, Al Cane, goes to Nice in *The Freeloaders* (1961)
to write a TV play for production in Europe. Lacy's
frequent bugaboo, Madison Avenue, cancels it at the
last minute, leaving Cane at loose ends, eventually to
get mixed up with several other Americans in a
robbery.

The cliché about writers being asked to "sell
out" is important to *Pity the Honest* (1965), the story
of Walt Moore, a hack writer for screen and
television magazines, and the first writer at the scene
of the death of Pat Riviera, "the most talented
performer ever." Walt gets involved with a group
similar to the so-called Frank Sinatra "ratpack" and as
a result has the opportunity for success in Las Vegas
and Hollywood, but he is not sure whether he is being
asked to cover up a murder.

Though they play relatively minor roles, two
writers in Lacy's work appear to be his surrogates.
Matt Tucker in *Go For the Body* was a reporter for
Stars and Stripes and has remained in Europe after
World War II. Tom Landy in *The Freeloaders* was a

correspondent for *Yank* (as was Lacy) and is now a reporter for the Paris-based *Herald-Tribune*. Though we learn little about him (or Tucker), Landy writes a newspaper story which is important to the plot. There is some evidence in Lacy's work that he regretted not having remained in Europe himself after the war.

The 1950s and 1960s were the "Golden Age" of paperback originals, but for most authors they were a time in which quantity was required to survive. The books Ed Lacy wrote during the two "careers" which sandwiched his hardcover books show many signs of a pressure to produce. Coincidences abound as a means of plot resolution, seen in some of Lacy's better books. Chance meetings are often crucial. An example occurs in *Go For the Body*, the lucky reunion of protagonist Ken Francine and the Italian woman with whom he worked while in the OSS during World War II. The accidental presence of a man and woman, now divorced, in the same large New York City apartment building is pivotal to *Bugged for Murder*. If two unrelated men who bear an uncanny resemblance did not have their paths cross in Manhattan, the story line in *Double Trouble*, one of Lacy's more weakly plotted books, would disappear. There is very little pedestrian traffic on Los Angeles streets, but two separate, random meetings on foot, both vital to the story, occur in *The Napalm Bugle*.

There are annoying, careless mistakes in Lacy, probably caused by haste. In *Enter Without Desire*, twilight in New York City occurs at 6:00 p.m. on a New Year's Eve, though at that time of year it would be well before 5:00 p.m. Sunflowers bloom in The Bronx in April in *In Black and Whitey*, though early August would be more accurate. A mistake in *The Napalm Bugle* is unconsciously funny as someone uses "buggering" rather than "bugging" in speaking of annoying another person. A tournament player in *Strip for Violence* is said to practice for matches mainly by hitting tennis balls against a wall, an implausibility to anyone familiar with the sport.

If mistakes and wild coincidences were originally Lacy's fault, they should have been caught by more careful editing. However, many of the paperbacks of Lacy's era received only cursory copy editing. (One exception was Gold Medal, a company that never published Lacy.) In Lacy's first book, his name is even misspelled "Lacey" on Avon's cover; the title page is correct. A reprint of *Moment of Untruth*, by Lodestone, has Toussaint Moore's name spelled "Toussiant" throughout. Surely a native New Yorker, like Lacy, would have corrected the spelling of "Reis" Park to "Riis" in *The Sex Castle*, given the opportunity.

The titles of Lacy's books were often poorly selected, ranging from the pedestrian, if accurate, *The Big Fix* to the misleading *Breathe No More, My Lady*. Often they were chosen, with little subtlety, to attract an audience looking for sex novels. How else can one explain *The Woman Aroused*, *Strip for Violence*, *Enter Without Desire*, *The Sex Castle*, and *The Big Bust*? Actually readers were not entirely misled since Lacy was one of the best erotic writers of his time. To paraphrase one of his own titles, Lacy created "The Male Reader Aroused" by sexual encounters, often with the woman as aggressor, plus vivid descriptions of women's figures and underwear. However, following the conventions of his era, he allowed room for the reader's imagination, without ever resorting to the 1970s graphic descriptions that caused well-established writer Henry Kane's paperbacks to be marketed as "X-Rated." Lacy was also forced to use euphemisms like "bull shine."

There is much repetition in Lacy, extending from people's names ("Wyckoff" is used as a last name in at least four books) to plot elements which recur frequently, including unhappy marriages and the pressures that writers face. Books are repeatedly padded without helping plot or character development. Almost every Lacy hero is described as a former boxer and/or football player who gets relaxation from driving cars.

Currently, none of Ed Lacy's work is in print, and that is unjustified even if it was inconsistent in quality, marked by strong and weak periods. An enterprising publisher should go through the Lacy *oeuvre*, selecting those works for reprint which would stand up. (Many are dated, but even that might be a plus with the current interest in nostalgia.) Three of his first five paperbacks, *Sin in Their Blood*, *Strip for Violence*, and *Go For the Body*, deserve a new audience. The first two would especially benefit from the resurgence of interest in the private eye.

Though some fans of paperback originals may disagree, the Lacy hardcover period must be considered his best. His plotting was far better than usual, and he avoided cliches and much of the repetition found in his poorer work. His characters were explored more deeply and are interestingly alive. With one exception, all of his hardcovers should be reprinted. His first hardcover, *The Best That Ever Did It* (1955), is told with freshness and vigor. Its hero, Barney Harris, is an auto-mechanic and a widower who becomes a private detective because the hours are more flexible and permit him to care for his school-age daughter. The murder of a policeman causes his widow to hire Harris, and he finds himself confronted by a case of police corruption and the first, and most clever, variation of several Lacy would ring on the theme of selling passports to people who cannot otherwise secure them.

Lacy wrote best about characters who were essentially good and with whom he and the reader

could identify. Marty Bond, in the hardcover *The Men
from the Boys* (1956), is the exception. He is a sleazy
ex-cop with two failed marriages, now a brutal, bigoted
hotel detective, not above pimping. Lacy makes Bond
interesting by giving him a serious stomach condition,
apparently cancer, and a believable reason to risk his
life so as not to prolong his agony.

Lead with Your Left and *Room to Swing*
introduced two well-realized series characters, Wintino
and Moore, who later appeared in paperback originals.
Each is good at his job, and each has conflicts in his
personal life which make him more believable.
Wintino's ambitious wife wants him to leave police
work and go into business. His feeling: "I'm not only
the youngest detective on the force, at the moment I'm
the *best*! That's important--I could never be the best
anything else" (page 161). Marcia Muller has called
Touie Moore "the first convincing black detective in
crime fiction" (in *1001 Midnights*, Arbor, 1986, pp. 456-
57) and that would have been true even had he not
appeared before the blander and incredibly stoic Virgil
Tibbs. Lacy knew his Harlem, and Moore's combination
home and office on 147th St. comes alive. The bigotry
he faces rings true and has the ability to infuriate the
reader. Yet Lacy, with Moore, avoided being preachy
or stacking the deck. A realistic touch is Moore
having trouble making ends meet as a detective, and
his girlfriend wanting him to take a safe, civil service
job as a mail carrier so they can get married. The
conflict of love of police work versus security and
ambition in the Moore and Wintino books is an age-old
one, and few in the mystery have presented it more
effectively than Ed Lacy.

There's hardly a likable character to be found in
Be Careful How You Live, Lacy's last mystery
hardcover, and it probably should not be reprinted.
It has a story-line right out of a sentimental 1930s
tear-jerker, with denied parenthood and other clichés.

The result is a melange of episodic writing in which
Lacy depends on coincidence to resolve his plot,
though he does include a nicely ironic ending, one of
many in his career. Incidentally, the main characters
are so uniformly obnoxious, and often stupid, that we
especially appreciate Wintino, who makes the equivalent
of a cameo appearance.

Though no longer being published in hardcover,
Lacy did some of his best paperback writing between
1958 and 1961. That was a peak period for paperback
originals, and Lacy's work compared favorably to that
of writers like John D. MacDonald and Dan J.
Marlowe. *Breathe No More, My Lady*, *The Big Fix*,
and *Bugged for Murder*, previously discussed, were all
strong. In an often forgotten book of the same time,
Shakedown for Murder, Lacy presented a hero off the
beaten track, an over-age New York City policeman,
widower Matt Lund, who has been relegated to being
little more than a jail custodian. On a Long Island
vacation, Matt finds a corpse, and his ego and desire
to impress his grandson cause him to use detective
skills he thought had atrophied.

The books Lacy set in exotic locations like the
Riviera, the South Pacific, Hollywood, Las Vegas, and
Mexico during the 1960s were his weakest. Books like
South Pacific Affair, *Two Hot to Handle*, and *The Sex
Castle* were about uninteresting, self-indulgent
characters who have run away from the kinds of gritty
situations about which Lacy wrote most effectively.

Novels in the 1960s also strayed from plausibility,
with doomsday situations and buried fascist treasures.
Previously, only in *Go For the Body* had Lacy
succumbed to this kind of plotting. He weakened what
otherwise was one of his better books by inserting a
mediocre Italian heavyweight who is being groomed as
another Mussolini, with plans to take over Italy.

In "Coin of Adventure," Kent Kelly, an American airplane pilot temporarily at loose ends in Northern Italy, is recruited in a scheme to find treasure Mussolini buried before he was captured. A group of neo-fascists is searching for the treasure, as are Leftists who want the list of Nazi collaborators that is buried with the treasure. One of Lacy's two posthumous novels, *The Big Bust*, is derivative of this novelette, involving an American private eye in Europe, recruited for a caper involving the rescue of buried Nazi treasure. O'Hara has already been unfaithful to his wife with one of Lacy's beautiful Amazons and summarizes his unlikely situation when he says,

> One day I'm merely a guy making a small buck shadowing wives or husbands, or devoting my time to something as earth-shaking as learning the details of a new model egg-beater for an industrial client. All that was less than a week ago and here I was, holding a rifle on a rugged Yugoslavian coast, where people had been ruthlessly slaughtered, with $60,000 pressing my gut and a chance of being a millionaire by tomorrow. Or dead. Plus old forty-four year old me had been part of one of the wildest sex bouts I'd ever imagined, even as a schoolboy dreamer (pages 129-130).

Perhaps it is unfair to Lacy, but one can speculate whether passages like that indicate the author was engaging in the kind of fantasy life that often goes with male menopause.

In Lacy's buried treasure stories, there is the resurgence of fascism, with dreams of world takeover. Doomsday is a lot closer in *The Napalm Bugle* because a problem of the rocket fuel we have been using forces the U.S. to change it simultaneously in all our missiles, leaving us totally defenseless and without operable missiles for twelve days. The defense establishment, of course, wants to keep that information secret. The unlikely plot has a left-wing British journalist witness the fuel failure and disappear. Only American pacifist Brad Armstrong is considered likely to find him. Surprisingly, he is asked for help by a right-wing Army general: ". . . this is a hawk and a dove having an emergency talk on the safety of the whole roost! I may be crazy to trust you, placing the security of our country on the line" (page 19). Published after *Fail-Safe* and *Seven Days in May*, Lacy's book does not have either the inner plausibility or the slick narrative qualities of either book. It is merely a trendy novel which hangs on the slimmest of premises, though once again Lacy almost rescues himself with a strong, ironic ending.

Perhaps most of all, for historical as well as entertainment values, Lacy's Lee Hays books deserve rescue from obscurity. *Harlem Underground* and *In Black and Whitey* superbly depict New York City as a powder keg, fearful of urban riot. They show a fine understanding of how to blend detective stories with events that could have come from the day's newspapers. They are told crisply with pace and bite. Lacy also displays considerable skill in portraying police officers in crisis as believable human beings. Because by the late 1960s speech was freer, Lacy was able to use language closer to what would be heard on urban streets.

Two decades have gone by since these books appeared and some of their appeal would be to a generation unaware of the 1960s riots, except as footnotes to American history. It is also good to make available books which can be read on two levels, as interesting mysteries and as superior fictionalized sociology. The much-publicized events in the Bernhard Goetz trial and the racially motivated death in Howard Beach, New York, in December 1986 suggest these books are still timely, since race

relations in the United States remain in danger of
return to the crises Lacy wrote of many years ago.

Checklist: Ed Lacy

Be Careful How You Live (Harper, 1958) (hardcover)
The Best That Ever Did It (Harper, 1955) (hardcover)
The Big Bust (Pyramid, 1969)
The Big Fix (Pyramid, 1960)
Breathe No More, My Lady (Avon, 1958)
Bugged for Murder (Avon, 1961)
Double Trouble (Lancer, 1967) (original publication
      in British hardcover: Boardman, 1965)
Enter Without Desire (Avon, 1954)
The Freeloaders (Berkley, 1961)
Go for the Body (Avon, 1954)
Harlem Underground (Pyramid, 1965)
Hold with the Hares (as Len Zinberg) (Doubleday,
      1948) (hardcover)
In Black and Whitey (Lancer, 1967)
Lead with Your Left (Harper, 1957) (hardcover)
      (quotes in text from 1958 Permabook reprint)
The Men from the Boys (Harper, 1956) (hardcover)
Moment of Untruth (Lancer, 1964)
The Napalm Bugle (Pyramid, 1968)
Pity the Honest (Macfadden, 1965) (original
      publication in British hardcover: Boardman, 1964)
Room to Swing (Harper, 1957) (hardcover)
The Sex Castle (Paperback Library, 1963)
Shakedown for Murder (Avon, 1958)
Sin in Their Blood (Eton, 1952)
Sleep in Thunder (Grosset and Dunlap, 1964)
South Pacific Affair (Belmont, 1961)
Strip for Violence (Eton, 1953)
Two Hot to Handle (Paperback Library, 1963)
Walk Hard--Talk Loud (as Len Zinberg) (Bobbs-Merrill,
      1940) (hardcover)
What D'ya Know for Sure (as Len Zinberg)
      (Doubleday, 1947) (hardcover)
The Woman Aroused (Avon, 1951)

JIM THOMPSON: THE KILLERS INSIDE HIM

by Max Allan Collins

Jim Thompson remains as anonymous a figure in American letters, even in that shabby corner of American letters known as mystery or crime fiction, as his name would suggest: a surname as common as Smith or Jones, a nickname as common as Joe or Jack, the sort of name the phone books are full of.

Even in the bylines of his two early attempts at mainstream novels, *Now and On Earth* (1942) and *Heed the Thunder* (1946), Thompson chose "Jim" over James. This might be viewed as a lack of pretension on the writer's part, or it might be seen as an affectation, a perverse reverse pretension. The continued use of the nickname throughout his career could also be part of Thompson's strategy, as the familiarity, the "just folks"-ness of Oklahoma Jim's crime novels, like their paperback format, serves to lower the expectations, and defenses, of the reader, who before long steps on a Thompson paragraph that hits him in the face like a loose board.

If the world were fair (and it isn't--if it were, Thompson would have had little to write about), Jim Thompson would today be as well known and as highly thought of as his literary progenitor, James M. Cain. It might be said that, roughly, Thompson is to Cain as Chandler is to Hammett. Like Chandler, Thompson has talent and skills worthy of his predecessor, but like Chandler, he brings them to bear on areas his predecessor did not explore. And, like Chandler's, Thompson's voice, his shading, is uniquely his own. Thompson, however, wasn't as limited an artist as

Chandler (who, good as he was, wrote one book seven times) and at times outstrips even Cain. This is not to suggest that Thompson is "better" than Cain (or Chandler or Hammett). It is, however, a suggestion that he is worthy of similar attention--and respect.

Obstacles have stood in the way of Thompson's achieving the status he deserves. For many years, not the least of these was the physical inaccessibility (in the United States, at least) of his work. Until very recently no Thompson book had been in print in this country for better than a decade--with the exception of *The Getaway* (1959), solely because it was the source of a Sam Peckinpah film and generated a 1973 "movie edition" paperback.

His novel *The Killer Inside Me* (1952) has long enjoyed a cult reputation, based largely on R. V. Cassill's famous essay in *Tough Guy Writers of the Thirties*, "Fear, Purgation, and the Sophoclean Light"; but it might still be safe to say that as many people have read about *The Killer Inside Me* as have read it.

It is not true, however, that Thompson enjoyed no critical success during his lifetime; several critics, including Anthony Boucher of the *New York Times,* championed his work. Also, he co-wrote two of Stanley Kubrick's earliest (and best) films, *The Killing* and *Paths of Glory*; and a number of his books have themselves generated films, most recently in Europe, notably the award-winning French film, *Coup de Torchon* (1981), directed by Bertrand Tavernier.

But in the United States, for many years Thompson has been best known by the crime fiction fans who collected the scarce, expensively "collectible" used copies of the original (and in most cases only) American printings of the novels--paperbacks mostly, the lion's share published by the obscure Lion Books.

With the exception of his one outright Cain imitation, the first-rate *Nothing More Than Murder* (Harper, 1949), all of Thompson's crime novels appeared as paperbacks and lack the legitimacy hardcover publication might have lent them--and him. His career, having been largely limited to the paperback ghetto, served to turn him into a literary curio, rather than a literary figure.

This has, to a degree, changed in recent years. Otto Penzler's trade paperback edition of *The Killer Inside Me* opened a Thompson floodgate, and a small California publisher, Creative Arts Books (under their Black Lizard imprint), has done a fine job of bringing many of Thompson's novels back into print as trade paperbacks sporting evocatively trashy covers. The 1986 publication by Donald Fine of *Hardcore*, an omnibus including *The Kill-Off*, *The Nothing Man* and *Bad Boy*, received many glowing reviews, including a full page in *Newsweek*.

Something of a Thompson bandwagon is momentarily careening along, just waiting for a lack of popular success to bump Thompson's novels back into the cult-favorite gutter. The first sign of trouble is the follow-up volume to *Hardcore*, entitled *More Hardcore*; that title indicates a hastiness that the contents and packaging further confirm. Unlike the first volume, *More Hardcore* has no perspective-setting introduction (the Black Lizard volumes help out their readers with before *and* after pieces). And the selection of novels reflects more seeming haste: *The Ripoff*, *Roughneck* and *The Golden Gizmo*, minor Thompsons all. *The Ripoff* is a posthumous novel that only the most dedicated Thompson fan could tolerate; a more casual reader deserves at least the guidance of an introduction. Reviews of *More Hardcore* have not been glowing.

Meanwhile, rumors have been flying that mass-

market editions of Thompson's entire list are in the
planning from a major publisher. This would, I'm
afraid, doom the Thompson bandwagon as surely as fate
damns a typical Thompson protagonist.

Despite his mass-market career, Thompson is not
a writer whose work is readily accessible to most
readers. For one thing, he is extremely uneven; his
craft was only occasionally up to his genius. For
another, his best books are unpleasant, hardly good
"summer reading," nothing Aunt Minnie would want to
curl up with on her beach towel.

Not everyone will find Jim Thompson's descents
into madness a trip worth taking; in this sense,
Thompson is to Cain as Spillane is to Chandler:
stronger, darker medicine, the violence and sex
starkly, unapologetically depicted, the protagonist's
mental state constantly verging on and often entering
into psychosis, all of which still causes the books of
both to be dismissed as trash when given a superficial
reading. Certainly anyone who finds Jim Cain
unpleasant will, upon encountering Jim Thompson, rush
for the exits almost immediately.

The subject matter of Thompson's best books is
so disturbing as to make Cain, the master of the
"tabloid murder," seem a friendly spinner of tales.
Cain, in his best three novels (*The Postman Always
Rings Twice*, *Double Indemnity* and *Serenade*),
leavened his bitter bread with a love story--a sordid
love story to be sure, but a love story.

This gave readers something to identify with,
even gave a roller-coaster thrill to the proceedings by
suggesting that love could drive a man and woman to
conspire to (and commit) murder together. This gave a
nobility to Cain's murderous adulterers. "It was like
being in church," *Postman*'s Frank Chambers says of
his love for married Cora. Love is bigger than right

or wrong: "Hell could have opened for me then, and it
wouldn't have made any difference. I had to have
her, if I hung for it." Cain, that failed opera singer,
was writing operas all along.

But occasionally he hinted at the madness that
Thompson would later embrace. In *Double Indemnity*,
the conclusion--insurance man-cum-murderer Walter
Huff prepares to commit an oddly ritualistic suicide
with black widow Phyllis Nirdlinger--suggests the
lunacy that Thompson would subject his readers to for
books at a time.

Thompson rarely gives the reader an easy time
of it; love as shabbily noble as Frank Chambers' and
Cora Papadakis' is a rarity in Thompson, and the
often quiet, but all-pervasive madness of Thompson's
protagonists is unrelenting once it's sneaked up on
you.

Not all of Jim Thompson books deal with
murderers or psychopaths as their protagonists, but
the best and most characteristic do. Among his other
works are the rambling, somewhat fanciful,
ancedotally autobiographical volumes, *Bad Boy* (1953)
and *Roughneck* (1954); the Caldwellesque *Cropper's
Cabin* (1952); and several modern-day westerns and
historical novels (*The Transgressors*, 1961; *South of
Heaven*, 1967; and *King Blood*, 1973). Several times he
flirts with the mainstream by dealing with social
concerns (alcoholism in *The Alcoholics*, 1953; racial
tension in *Child of Rage*, 1972), but his quirky, surreal,
blackly humorous treatment of such subjects relegates
him to the paperback ghetto. Obviously, though, he
had range and could be a solid professional workhorse
when necessary, as evidenced by the somewhat
demeaning movie and TV novelizations he turned to
late in his career.

Thompson seems to have been a writer who

worked fast, in a white heat, with little or no rewriting; and what served him best was a first-person narrative, in which he could "plot by the seat of his pants" and follow his disturbed protagonists wherever their warped personalities and streams of consciousness happened to flow. First and most famous of these generally amiable psychopaths is Lou Ford, Deputy of Central City (population around 50,000), the "hero" of *The Killer Inside Me*.

Ford pretends to be a rather simple-minded, cliché-spouting hick, the sort of dopey bore anybody hates to be cornered by; but Ford is actually a cunning, complex, even brilliant psycho who is playing cat-and-mouse with the world, having his little joke on all of us. Thompson has his joke by revealing Ford's madness a little at a time, allowing us to be fooled by him for a while ourselves. Ford is an untrustworthy narrator, but he doesn't lie to the reader so much as to himself.

The sexual relationships in *The Killer Inside Me* are sadomasochistic, and the women characters are not entirely convincing--one key character, Joyce Lakeland, makes too short an appearance to make her proper impact on the story. Better realized is Amy, who does have a genuine love for Ford, which he recognizes in alternately appreciative and contemptuous narrative ramblings; she suspects Ford may be a murderer, but risks it and dies for her faith in him and humanity. In a particularly nasty--and effective--narrative ploy, Thompson has Ford tell us at the start of the chapter that he has killed Amy, then backtracks and painstakingly details everything for the two weeks leading up to that brutal murder, including their lovemaking ("We had two weeks, and they were pretty good ones").

What is frightening about all of this--for the reader strong enough of mind and stomach to go the distance--is that Ford (and most later Thompson psychopath/narrators) never becomes completely unsympathetic. In Cain, the protagonist is a poor schmuck whose fantasies about making it with the boss's wife come sordidly true; and the web the protagonist gets caught up in seems at least vaguely religious--maybe God's behind it, or the devil, or just plain old Fate. In Thompson, the protagonist is driven to violent acts that seldom make the sort of "sense" of a Cain plot, with its motivations in greed and love. Lou Ford kills because he has "the sickness."

In Thompson, "fate" is defined as environment and heredity ganging up on you. There is no master plan, no web of destiny, not even karma, to give sense to life; there are just "circumstances" beyond our control that form us. And some of us, like Lou Ford, are misshapen.

At the close of *The Killer Inside Me* there is a sort of prayer, which is Thompson at his best:

And they all lived happily ever after, I guess, and I guess--that's--all.

Yeah, I reckon that's all unless our kind gets another chance in the Next Place. Our kind. Us people.

All of us that started the game with a crooked cue, that wanted so much and got so little, that meant so good and did so bad. All us folks. Me and Joyce Lakeland, and Johnnie Pappas and Bob Maples and big ol' Elmer Conway and little ol' Amy Stanton. All of us.

All of us.

Of course the people listed in Ford's dying prayer are his own murder victims.

Ford also appears in *Wild Town* (1957), a sequel to *The Killer Inside Me*; an interesting book, it provides a third-person look at Lou Ford, the psychopath viewed from outside. And Thompson confirms our suspicions of Lou Ford: "Ford's clownish mannerisms were too exaggerated, no more than a mask for a coldly calculating and super-sharp mind."

Unfortunately, the book is otherwise lower-drawer Thompson. He is seldom at his best in the third person. The protagonist is David "Bugsy" McKenna, a stubborn, bad-tempered and not terribly bright drifter who becomes house detective at the Hanlon Hotel. The oil-rich Oklahoma "wild town" of the title is mostly off-stage, as McKenna's troubles are largely confined to the somewhat seedy hotel; but a real sense of Deputy Ford's corrupt hold on the town is conveyed nonetheless.

Wild Town is something of a mystery--McKenna is accidentally involved in a death for which he's being blackmailed, and seeks the blackmailer's identity --and Ford is, oddly enough, something of a detective by book's end. But this unusual novel remains only a footnote to its better-known predecessor, and is characterized by some of Thompson's most meandering, careless plotting.

Thompson's psychopaths have much in common, but each is distinct. The closest Thompson comes to repeating himself is in *Pop. 1280* (1964), whose protagonist Nick Corey bears a great deal of resemblance to Lou Ford. Like Ford, he's a law officer (a sheriff) and, like Ford, he feigns folksy stupidity while committing cunning, vile and often pointless murders, using his position as sheriff to cover them up. The setting is a small Southern river town before the turn of the century, and the flavor is at once reminiscent of Erskine Caldwell and Mark Twain;

the latter influence is such that Corey at times seems
a psychopathic Huck Finn.   Thompson is at his best
here--on familiar ground, he seems almost to be
having fun, not trying as hard as he did in the
sometimes uneven telling of Lou Ford's story; *Pop.
1280*, a reworking of his most famous book, may be his
best book.

This is partially because *Pop. 1280* is a black
comedy; *Killer Inside Me* is far too bleak for Lou
Ford's absurd behavior to approach the black humor
that pervades the later novel.   Corey seems so picked
on and put upon (by his shrewish wife Myra, among
others) that the reader begins to root for this
combination Li'l Abner/William Heirens.

Also, the reader initially underestimates Corey--
just as have the other characters in the novel.   By the
end, Corey has come to the conclusion that he is Jesus
Christ.   (". . . why else had I been put here in Potts
county, and why else did I stay here?   Why else, who
else, what else but Christ Almighty would put up with
it?")   He also concludes that being Christ doesn't seem
to be to any particular advantage.

Behind Thompson's black humor here, of course,
is the notion that the human condition is so
unpleasant as to drive each of us mad, at least a
little.   And perhaps, after identifying with or at least
allowing ourselves to be confined within the point of
view of a madman, we will understand the madness of,
say, Richard Speck--and the madness in ourselves--a
little better.

There is compassion in Thompson's vision; there is
a sadness behind it, and a longing for, but deep doubt
in, an afterlife.   The title of the Thompson novella
This World, Then the Fireworks, is a direct, wry
reference to Thompson's view of life and the hereafter,
an empty promise of something better, something

exciting, after we trudge through this vale of tears.
Are the promised "fireworks" hell?   Heaven?
Nothingness,   more   likely--Thompson's   narrator
describes a graveyard as "The City of Wonderful
People."

       The novel in which Thompson's compassion is
most obvious is *The Nothing Man* (1954). Alcoholic
reporter   Clint   Brown   is   a   vintage   Thompson
psychopath, whose "sickness" is a result of his having
been castrated in the war.   His current newspaper
editor happens to be the wartime captain who sent him
into battle and cost him his manhood.   In this, one of
his most harrowing novels, Thompson paints a picture
of a blackout drunk who seems to have committed (and
actually attempts) several murders; at the conclusion,
however,   the   protagonist,   through   the   wildest   of
coincidences, is revealed to be not *technically* guilty of
the crimes (for example, a sleeping woman he "kills"
turns out to have already been dead, a suicide victim
by overdose). This allows Thompson one of his rare,
uncharacteristic "happy" endings, in which he suggests
that the protagonist will pull himself up and out of his
mental state and alcoholism into a better, more normal
life.   After taking us on one of his bleakest rides,
Thompson presents a wholly unconvincing rosy finish,
seriously   damaging   one   of   his   most   interesting,
revealing works.

       Thompson's endings frequently give him trouble;
he seems to thrash around, but that thrashing around
sometimes   leads   to   something   brilliant   (as   in   the
concluding "prayer" of *Killer Inside Me*). Still, some of
his best novels are at least a little flawed by uncertain
conclusions.   In *The Grifters* (1963), the problem of
The Nothing Man's finale is reversed: a largely upbeat
story about a young con artist is shattered by a
"surprise" downbeat conclusion. This conclusion is at
least consistent with Thompson's world: the mother
whose upbringing of her son sent him into a life of

crime kills him, accidentally--fate as circumstance, destiny as heredity, and environment mindlessly conspiring to our oblivion.

Thompson's own alcoholism obviously had much to do with *The Nothing Man*, but an earlier novel made an even more direct approach. *The Alcoholics* (1953) is one of Thompson's worst books, a black comedy that rambles plotlessly through a day and night at El Healtho sanitorium. It is the heavy-handed and frequently incoherent tale of Dr. Peter S. Murphy's efforts to raise funds for the institution, as well as his relationship with a beautiful, sadistic nurse named Lucretia Baker. Miss Baker has a lisp, which the author seems to find amusing--as a writer of dialogue, Thompson is at his worst and most mean-spirited when depicting speech defects and dialects. The nurse's sadism, if not her lisp, is cured when Dr. Murphy good-naturedly rapes her, which she of course comes to enjoy. ("You thilly, thilly man!")

At the close of *The Alcoholics*, however, Thompson inserts a telling vignette: a drunken writer checks in at the clinic. "Just the man," Dr. Murphy says, "to write a book about this place."

In the same year the unfortunate *Alcoholics* appeared (1953), Thompson also published *Savage Night*, a brilliant, little-discussed novel that surpasses *Killer Inside Me* and rivals *Pop. 1280*.

Charlie (Little) Bigger, now calling himself Carl Bigelow, a diminutive hitman, comes to a small college town and poses as a nice, innocent college boy while planning a murder. Bigger/Bigelow is at the end of the road: dying of T.B., slowly. He falls in love with a crippled girl, Ruthie; their mutual deformities (he views his shortness as such) link them in his mind. After an adulterous affair with his landlady (his potential victim's wife, no less), Bigelow hopes for

something better, something pure, with Ruthie, who
turns out to be in the employ of "the Man," Bigelow's
boss, and in fact has been keeping an eye on the little
killer. The would-be lovers end up in a secluded house
with a yard overgrown with weeds; in a succession of
short chapters, Thompson tells of their isolation and
increasing madness, as Bigelow hides in the basement
only to be attacked by Ruthie, who chops him up with
an axe. This Thompson has Bigelow relate in the first
person:

> She was swinging wild. My right shoulder
> was hanging by a thread, and the spouting
> forearm dangled from it. And my scalp, my
> scalp and the left side of my face was dangling
> . . . and . . . and I didn't have a nose . . . or
> chin . . . or . . .

Bigelow crawls around the basement, though
"there was hardly any of me" left, and meets Death:
"And he smelled good."

This is clearly out of Cain's *Double Indemnity*
conclusion, but there is a madness and poetry here
only hinted at in Cain; Thompson leaps into lunacy,
and drags his readers along, like it or not. The
result is, oddly enough, rewarding and even moving.
What makes *Savage Night* one of Thompson's most
powerful works is the more overtly sympathetic
Bigelow, whose actions are never as psychotic or
sadistic as Lou Ford's or even Nick Corey's; he is a
victim (with all of us) of the human condition.

Not all of Thompson's first-person protagonists
are killers. Several of his novels are rather
straightforward crime stories, often involving scams of
one sort or another, as is the case in *Recoil* (1953), in
which a good-natured young ex-con maneuvers his way
out of the machinations of corrupt politicians and the
like and into a relatively happy (and convincing)

ending.

Texas By The Tail (1965) features another good-natured protagonist, a con man/gambler who is deeply in love with his shapely, red-headed accomplice, though haunted by an earlier unsuccessful marriage, about which the accomplice does not know. A number of chapter openings feature wryly witty travelogues as the duo moves across the southwest, and the book boasts a fine psychological study of the con man--and a complete absence of any moralizing point of view from the author about his protagonist's profession. Thompson's plotting and structure are haphazard, however, making *Texas By The Tail* a fast-moving vehicle on its way to no place in particular.

Occasionally Thompson uses third person, as in *A Swell Looking Babe* (1954), in which a conniving bellboy's good looks and boyish charm lead him into a murder scheme and an unhappy (and pat) ending. This story introduces a Columbo-like lawyer, Kossmeyer, who turns up in several other Thompson novels, always in a minor but significant role.

The Getaway is a deftly-plotted third-person crime novel that foreshadows Richard Stark's Parker series and has an ironic, bleak conclusion that the strangely sterile Peckinpah adaptation, a bloody but bloodless film, omits. *The Getaway* is Thompson's finest third-person novel and may well be his finest hour as a craftsman; still, it lacks the impact of the first-person narration found in even his lesser novels.

In one such novel, *The Kill-Off* (1957), the story is related in the first person but each chapter is told from the point of view of a different character. This ambitious book attempts to merge the crime novel with a *Peyton Place*-style tale, unsuccessfully.

Thompson had tried this narrative trick earlier,

and more successfully, in *The Criminal* (1953). An
innocent young girl is raped and murdered, and her
equally young and innocent boy-next-door friend is
suspected; society's hypocrisy on all levels is savagely
searched out by the author, whose compassion is
limited largely to the two young people. But
Thompson's ending is again hasty and out of left field;
and the lack of focus inherent in his multiple first-
person viewpoints makes this an ambitious but minor
work.

   The Kill-Off and *The Criminal* are further linked
by the appearance in both of the Kossmeyer
character.

   The Golden Gizmo (1954) careens between
melodrama and comedy, and fizzles out into neither;
but one effective plot device--the protagonist thinks
he's killed his wife, but she turns up alive much later
--makes the novel memorable. Also, like Cain,
Thompson often uses the realistic, well-researched
portrayal of a profession as a backdrop for his stories;
in *Nothing More Than Murder*, for example, it's the
film rental business. In *The Golden Gizmo*, it's gold-
buying, of the door-to-door variety. *Gizmo* also boasts
Thompson's most arresting opening sentence: "It was
almost quitting time when Toddy met the man with no
chin and the talking dog."

   The Ripoff (1987, published posthumously) is
undoubtedly Thompson's worst novel; it makes a
reader long for *The Alcoholics*. The premise is clever
enough--the protagonist must solve the mystery of
who is trying to kill him--but the execution is dismal,
wavering uncertainly between comedy and crime novel.
The thick-as-a-brick protagonist, who seems to get a
great deal of enjoyment watching his two girlfriends
urinate (not at the same time fortunately), is caught
up in the most haphazardly plotted Thompson tale of
them all (much of it a recycling of *Texas By The Tail*

elements), with an ending that would make a shaggy dog groan. This one is very reminiscent of the several posthumously published James M. Cain novels, although much their inferior.

Let me interrupt myself to make the point that I am much in *favor* of the unpublished novels of the likes of Thompson and Cain seeing the posthumous light of day. But such books must be presented with care, and must (as was the case with the Mysterious Press editions of posthumous Cain novels) be skillfully edited. Having edited and prepared for publication the Thompson novella *This World, Then the Fireworks*, I know all too well the need to protect the reputations of such authors by giving them proper editing and presentation. Thompson wrote quickly, offhandedly. He needed a strong editor. It's clear that such editors as Arnold Hano and Knox Burger served him well.

A Hell of a Woman (1954) is perhaps the best example of Thompson's offhanded brilliance. His protagonist, Frank Dillon, is a door-to-door salesman, an innocuous sort, apparently not terribly bright. Initially, at least, the prose seems as undistinguished as the protagonist: "she was wearing a white wrap-around," Dillon tells us, "the sort of get-up you see on waitresses and lady barbers. The neck of it came down in a deep *V*, and you could see she had plenty of what it takes in that area." Gradually, however, we become aware that this typical Thompson blue-collar "hero" isn't always telling us the truth. Soon he's relating the story of how he met his wife Joyce, only to interject, "No, now wait a minute," as he realizes the anecdote may actually be about his previous wife; or is it the one before that . . . ?

Dillon, alternately shrewd and bumbling, allows himself to be drawn into a scheme to murder a young woman's sadistic aunt, who has apparently been forcing "innocent" Mona to prostitute herself. The old woman

has a stash of cash--$100,000--and Dillon conspires
with Mona to do the old lady in for it. In James M.
Cain this might make for a tidy, if twisting, plot; in
Thompson, the twists are decidedly untidy, as Dillon
experiences difficulties with his boss at the Pay-E-Zee
Store and with his on-again-off-again wife and even
with Mona, who seems to be nothing more than a
common prostitute after all.

The self-pitying narrator whines and schemes
and, eventually, kills--several times, in a cold-
blooded fashion that would do Lou Ford proud.
Especially disturbing is the friendly relationship Dillon
strikes up with a man he intends to (and later does)
kill, purely to advance his and Mona's machinations;
and one soul-chilling moment has Dillon given the news
by his wife Joyce that she's pregnant with his child
just as he's about to murder her (and does).

A preposterous, bold plot twist near the end of
the book has the murdered aunt turning out to be a
retired Ma Barker type who had kidnapped Mona as a
child. The $100,000 is Mona's kidnap ransom, it seems,
and the money is marked, leading to the downfall of
all concerned. At the bitter end, Dillon is on the run
and mired in booze, hard drugs and harder women, and
in an odd, experimental final chapter, Thompson
alternates lines of narrative, every other line in italics,
giving two concurrent but somewhat contradictory (yet
equally frightening) accounts of what seem to be
Dillon's final moments--final moments that may
include castration and/or suicide.

In moments like these, Thompson can seem as
desperate as his characters, groping for an ending,
but *A Hell of a Woman*'s finale manages to skirt
incoherence and leaves the reader breathless, if
confused, wondering if Thompson is a genius, a
madman, or both.

painfully coy ones with Lois, into fully-realized scenes
with fully-realized characters. Thompson was certainly
capable of that.

But he chose not to in *This World, Then the
Fireworks*; nonetheless, its strengths outweigh its
weaknesses--particularly for any reader with a special
interest in this unjustly if understandably neglected
author. This short novel is a typical, if not shining,
example of what Thompson did best: force the reader
into the tortured psyche of a soul whose "sickness" is
cloaked in superficial normalcy. Sometimes, as with
Lou Ford and Nick Corey, the spouting of cliches
creates the mask; in the case of Martin Lakewood, his
native intelligence and charm create a facade.

Intellectual and philosophical pretensions like
Marty's are common among Thompson narrators--
including Lou Ford in his non-folksy moments--and
seem derived, in part, from the similar pretensions of
Ralph Cotter, the college-educated narrator of Horace
McCoy's 1948 novel, *Kiss Tomorrow Goodbye*, which
appears to be as much a precursor to Thompson as
anything in Cain.

What is most impressive about *This World, Then
the Fireworks* is the brother/sister motif; and the
horrific, yet poetic opening, echoed in the situation
(and in one key paragraph) at the novel's conclusion,
is haunting and effective. The childhood trauma
inflicted on both Martin and Carol grants them
Thompson's understanding and compassion.

Or, as Marty himself puts it: ". . . everyone is as
he is for sound reasons, because circumstance has so
formed him."

And:

We were culpable, I said, only to the

degree that all life, all society, was culpable.
We were no more than the pointed instruments
of that life, activated symbols in an allegory
whose authors were untold billions.

Checklist: Jim Thompson

After Dark, My Sweet (Popular Library, 1955)
The Alcoholics (Lion, 1953)
Bad Boy (Lion, 1953)
Child of Rage (Lancer, 1972)
The Criminal (Lion, 1953)
Cropper's Cabin (Lion, 1952)
Fireworks (Fine, 1988) (hardcover short story
    collection)
The Getaway (Signet, 1959)
The Golden Gizmo (Lion, 1954)
The Grifters (Regency, 1963)
Hardcore (Fine, 1986) (hardcover omnibus)
Heed the Thunder (Greenberg, 1946) (hardcover)
A Hell of a Woman (Lion, 1954)
The Kill-Off (Lion, 1957)
The Killer Inside Me (Lion, 1952)
King Blood (Sphere, 1973) (published in U.S. in
    1954 under unidentified title per Hubin, *Crime
    Fiction, 1749-1980*)
More Hardcore (Fine, 1987) (hardcover omnibus)
The Nothing Man (Dell, 1954)
Nothing More Than Murder (Harper, 1949) (hardcover)
Now and On Earth (Modern Age, 1942) (hardcover)
Pop. 1280 (Gold Medal, 1964)
Recoil (Lion, 1953)
Roughneck (Lion, 1954)
Savage Night (Lion, 1953)
South of Heaven (Gold Medal, 1967)
A Swell-Looking Babe (Lion, 1954)
Texas by the Tail (Gold Medal, 1965)
The Transgressors (Signet, 1961)
Wild Town (Signet, 1957)

THE NOVELS OF VIN PACKER

by Jon L. Breen

Today, any type of mystery novel from the toughest to the coziest might be published first in paperback. The paperback original of the nineteen-fifties, however, was almost entirely a hardboiled, masculine domain, directed at a male audience and created by male writers. Not until the contemporary gothic trend of the sixties and seventies did female-oriented mystery fiction become a major factor in original softcover form. There is at least one exception, however, to the overwhelming maleness of the major paperback original writers of the fifties: Vin Packer, who is unique among the most successful paperback writers of the decade in other ways as well.

Vin Packer was born Marijane Meaker in Auburn, New York, in 1927. Though she has used her birth name as a byline occasionally, notably on the novel *Shockproof Sydney Skate* (1972), the bulk of her work has appeared pseudonymously. Her best-known pen name is M. E. Kerr, which she has used for a highly successful and honored group of young adult novels, beginning with *Dinky Hocker Shoots Smack* (1972).

M. E. Kerr's autobiography, *Me Me Me Me Me* (Harper and Row, 1983), discusses her early life through her sale of a short story (under the name Laura Winston) to *Ladies' Home Journal* in 1951. The book is addressed to the readers of her young adult novels and refers frequently to characters she used in the M. E. Kerr titles, but there are occasional references to her work as Vin Packer, including her possibly unique reason for entering the suspense field:

"solely because I'd heard that *The New York Times*' mystery columnist, Anthony Boucher, would review paperbacks. Encouraged by his reviews of my work, I stayed in the field about ten years before going on to hardcover under my own name, Meaker" (page 212).

As the quote above suggests, Packer's original impulse as a novelist was not building either puzzles or suspense. Very few of her books can accurately be called detective or mystery stories, though they are certainly crime novels. Most are not even suspense tales in the conventional sense. Rather, they are straight novels that happen to concern a crime, and usually the action consists of the events leading up to the crime, with the emphasis on the criminal's motivation. Once the crime has taken place, the novel is virtually over. The investigation rarely plays a major part.

A number of elements recur again and again in Packer's fiction. One of the most pervasive is the troubled adolescent character. Though many of the later novels deal entirely with adults, equally troubled, the interest in the problems of youth that would inspire the M. E. Kerr books is quite obvious in the early Packers. Her ability to get inside the heads of children and teenagers, realistically reflecting their problems and attitudes, is comparable to Stephen King's. More than once, the central character is an adolescent male being raised by a widowed or divorced mother, with a well-meaning but ineffectual family friend attempting to serve as father substitute.

Another recurring element is homosexuality. Under the name Ann Aldrich, Packer wrote paperback Lesbian novels, a surprisingly viable sub-genre in the fifties, though there was no comparable market for sympathetic stories of male homosexuality, at least from mainstream publishers. Some of the Packer novels have specifically gay subject matter, and references to homosexuality, veiled and direct, are numerous even in those that do not.

References to college days are frequent, with much attention to the initiation and rushing rites of fraternities and sororities. Many characters share Packer's background at the University of Missouri, specifically its vaunted journalism school.

Packer often employs quotations from popular song lyrics (oddly, never with a copyright notice) and poetry, sometimes original. The novels are always *au courant*, filled with topical references to news events, motion picture and television personalities, and concerns of the day.

Finally, and most significantly, Packer's novels are totally devoid of either heroes or villains. Virtually everyone is troubled, mixed up, or deluded at best, psychotic at worst. No one is totally okay, and nearly every character has at least some redeeming qualities. Packer specializes in psychopathic killers of varying types, and her treatment of them is never simplistic. Indeed, her absolute refusal to provide easy answers to psychological or social problems is one of the qualities that most endeared her to the critic she originally sought to impress, Anthony Boucher.

Come Destroy Me (1954) was not the first Vin Packer novel. Gold Medal, the publisher of all but one of Packer's paperback originals, lists three earlier books opposite the title page. *Spring Fire*, a Lesbian-themed book published in 1952, was her first major success and perhaps her most famous single title of the period. Also listed are *Dark Intruder* (1952) and *Look Back on Love* (1953), both of which are identified as crime fiction in Allen J. Hubin's bibliography, *Crime Fiction, 1749-1980*. But *Come Destroy Me* was the first of her books to be reviewed by Boucher and the

earliest I have examined for this article. It sets a
pattern for many of the Packer suspense novels to
come. Only from the publisher's cover blurb and the
chapter epigraphs would the reader know until very
late in the story that the book was a crime novel.
Packer is interested in exploring the roots of violent
crime, and most of the novel is concerned with setting
up the circumstances that eventually lead to murder.

The setting of *Come Destroy Me* is Azrael,
Vermont, in the Green Mountains. Sixteen-year-old
Charlie Wright is a quiet library habitue, a brilliant,
Harvard-bound student who is constantly teased by his
college-age sister Evie. Most prominent older male
figure in the fatherless household is irritating lawyer-
widower Russel Lofton, who is mildly courting
Charlie's mother, Emily. Epigraphs from trial
testimony and psychiatric reports let us know that
Charlie will kill, but the suspense lies in whom, how,
and why. Although the reader knows Charlie will do
murder, he initially doesn't seem all that much more
troubled and confused than most adolescents, and
therein lies much of the case history's fascination.

Object of Charlie's sexual fantasy is book dealer
Jill Latham. Their first meeting foreshadows the
classic coming-of-age movie *Summer of '42*, though this
meeting is considerably less innocent on both sides.
Jill is an odd-mannered heavy drinker with affected
speech patterns, very much like a Tennessee Williams
character.

Boucher was immediately impressed. As he would
later, he praised Packer's reluctance to offer easy
answers--"she never quite answers her own questions
with any pat psychiatric diagram." The novel is "well
and subtly written, with acutely overhead [*sic*]
dialogue, full-length characterizations in brief compass,
and excerpts from hearings that capture the exact
flavor of authentic transcripts" (*New York Times Book*

Review, 7 March, 1954, page 27).

Whisper His Sin (1954), though very different in cast and milieu, follows a similar pattern. New Yorker Ferris Sullivan--a poetry reader, personally fastidious, a "hopeless eccentric"--arrives at Jackson University in Virginia. He is clearly homosexual, though the term is waltzed around in the first part of the novel. His mother has tried throughout his life to erase those "tendencies," also seen in his Uncle Arnold. At Jackson, senior Paul Lasher becomes Ferris's protector and the wealthy Carter Fryman IV his chief tormentor. Again, the chapter epigraphs foreshadow the crime to come, though the questions of who will be killer and who victim are more ambiguous. (As is often the case, Gold Medal's blurb tells far too much.)

The treatment of homosexuality in the novel is fascinating, since the author is apparently trying to satisfy the moral qualms of the public and depict gays sympathetically at the same time. Lasher, a closet homosexual who wants to be "double gaited," takes Sullivan to a gay party at a New York apartment, then is angry when Sullivan, for the first time in his life not an outsider, fits in with this world all too well. The host is a Capote-ish outward queen known as Rug (because people walk all over him). At the party, the discussion of the homosexual and his options in a straight society becomes franker. Of the guests, only a Merchant Marine, a very minor character, seems well-adjusted to his sexual identity, so this is not what the present-day gay community would be likely to hail as a "positive" depiction. Still, in a mass market 1954 paperback, the scene seems far ahead of its time.

Packer appealed to Anthony Boucher's keen interest in true crime cases. His review identified the murder with a "startling recent New York parricide" and described the book as "a forceful and tragic novel of college life, homosexuality (handled with a

surprising combination of good taste and explicitness),
and the bitter after-the-fact relationship between
collaborators in murder" (*NYTBR*, 31 October, 1954,
page 39).

Following two more novels of troubled youth,
The Thrill Kids (1955) and *The Young and the Violent*
(1956), both centered in New York, Packer published
the first of two novels concerned with race relations
in the deep South.

In the opening pages of *Dark Don't Catch Me*
(1956), Harlem youth Millard Post is sent unwillingly to
Paradise, Georgia. His grandmother is reported to be
dying, and his father can't get off work to make the
trip. As Millard travels south, and is gradually
introduced to the horrors and inconsistencies of Jim
Crow, we are filled in on the explosive situation that
awaits him, all revolving around the household of
wealthy landholder Thad Hooper: his long-dead twin
sister, his sexy wife, his children, his black servants,
and his white friends and neighbors, who are all busy
debating the implications of Brown versus the Board of
Education of Topeka, the Supreme Court decision
mandating school integration. More than anything else,
however, the large cast of black and white characters
is obsessed with and motivated by one thing: sex.

This time, all the specific foreshadowing of
crime is in the cover copy rather than the text.
Even more than its predecessors, this is a straight
novel for most of the distance. Like all Packer's
work, the novel is ambiguous and lacking in easy
answers, but it is less successful than *Come Destroy
Me* or *Whisper His Sin*. The reader has the feeling
that the eventual crime and its aftermath could have
been treated in greater detail--indeed, the story could
support a book twice the length. It could have been
an interesting example of the Big Trial novel, but
legal proceedings were usually employed by Packer

only in her chapter headings.

The overemphasis on sex brought the first mildly negative notice from Anthony Boucher, who found the book "dominated and distorted by an obsession with sex so powerful as to make John O'Hara's view of life seem somewhat bowdlerized." Packer made the root of "the entire Problem of the South . . . purely sexual in origin" (*NYTBR*, 21 December, 1956, page 12). The anonymous reviewer in *The Saint Detective Magazine*, which reviewed paperback original novels in a monthly feature called "The Saint's Ratings," awarded the novel two halos (the next to highest rating) but groused that the novel "tries to take the 'color problem' into a barely modernized Uncle Tom's Cabin. Outstanding craftsmanship is wasted on what any Southerner will recognize as strictly Yankee plumbing" (June 1957, page 111). Both reviews referred to the story's origin in a recent real-life case, pegged by Boucher the "wolf-whistle" case.

3 Day Terror (1957) has several similarities to its predecessor, being set in a small southern town (Bastrop, Alabama), also faced with the imminent integration of its schools and also visited by someone from New York. Dee Benjamin, who once had a celebrated local romance with editor Jack Chadwick, now returns from the North a divorcee. Stranger Richard Buddy is in town to campaign against school integration. His racist tracts consist of a chilling burlesque of songs from *My Fair Lady*. The novel continues the previous book's theme: that virtually all the racial troubles in the South are based on lust and sexual fear. Again, the body of the book is a build-up to a violent finish, but a less criminous one than in the earlier novels. Boucher did not review the book, and the *Saint's* rater awarded only one halo, while introducing similar caveats: "We fail to recognize too clearly Vin Packer's South and her Southern dialect seems to have a faint ring of the north in it. The story itself seems at times to get as confused as the lives of the people who tread not too ably through it" (December 1957, page 101).

The novel is clearly not one of Packer's best, but it contains the kind of social observation that makes the least of her work worthy of attention, as when politico Troy Porter discourses on the requirements for a southern politician: "Even God himself had to produce a son to get some respect down here, and a good politician's got to do a hell of a lot more. He's got to go to church, and he'd better have gone to war. He's got to have a wife, kids, a dog and a low-priced car. He can't get caught sinning, but he better seem capable of it" (page 27).

Packer's next novel, *5:45 to Suburbia* (1958), seems to be guiding the reader to a shock ending that never happens. Though listed with Packer's crime novels in Hubin's bibliography, it really isn't a crime novel at all but rather a combination of two fifties bestseller genres: the executive-suite novel and the adultery novel. Despite the title, there is very little about life in the suburbs. Main character is 50-year-old publishing executive Charlie Gibson, who objects to his company's new *Confidential*-type scandal magazine, yet unnamed but called *Vile* around the office. We meet Charlie on his fiftieth birthday, then flash back to earlier birthdays, beginning with his eighteenth when he was a student at the University of Missouri. A former classmate, now a TV commentator, is scheduled for exposé in *Vile* concerning an old pederasty charge.

Another 1958 book, *The Evil Friendship*, is definitely criminous, fictionalizing New Zealand's Parker-Hulme case of four years before. In his review, Boucher characterized the case as a Lesbian Loeb-Leopold and pronounced Packer "as relentlessly

tough-minded as any of the best 'hard-boiled' writers"
(*NYTBR*, 7 September, 1958, page 28).

The Twisted Ones (1959) may be the finest of
Packer's novels. The narrative alternates the lives of
three troubled youths: Brock Brown, 15, handsome,
puritanical New Yorker, a compulsive thief subject to
blinding headaches; Charles Berrey, 8, a precocious
New Jersey boy who is a big-money quiz show
contestant; and Reginald Whittier, 19, a shy stutterer,
mother-dominated with a friend-of-the-family father
substitute. Parents in Packer novels are full of well-
meant but excruciatingly harmful advice. Whittier's
mother exhorts him, "Be a bush if you can't be a tree!"

All three boys have serious problems, though
Brock is the most obviously disturbed, and in the
closing chapters all three commit murder. Though the
trio of well-drawn central characters never meet, they
are linked by Packer in inventive ways, and a
simplistic *Time*-style epilogue about Memorial day
murders by members of the "shook-up" generation
ironically brings them together at the end.

Though the novel was written before the quiz
scandals hit, the quiz-show sequences in *The Twisted
Ones* provide a good example of Packer's ability to
use the events that define the times in a way that is
successful both artistically and commercially. Her
next novel, *The Girl on the Best Seller List* (1960),
was inspired by another phenomenon of the day:
Grace Metalious and her best-selling novel of small-
town scandal, *Peyton Place*. In this novel, Packer
flirts with the whodunit form for the first time, as
several residents of Cayuta, New York, have good
reason to contemplate the murder of novelist Gloria
Whealdon, author of the best-selling *roman à clef,
Population 12,360*. What makes the subject matter
especially interesting is that Packer, though obviously
a more serious and admirable writer than the fictional

Whealdon (and probably the real-life Metalious), admits to drawing freely on real people and experiences for her own fiction. Typically, the expected crime occurs very late in the book. Though Packer answers the question of who committed the crime, there is a fine irony in the solution.

Both *Twisted Ones* and *Girl on the Best Seller List* have a character named Dr. Mannerheim. His first name changes from Clyde to Jay, but in each case he is a Ph.D. who practices or wants to practice psychology. Clyde has an art history doctorate but teaches psychology at Brock Brown's school. Jay actually practices psychology, but much is made of the fact that he is not a "real" doctor, and there is some question whether his bills can be taken as income-tax deductions. In a later Packer novel, *Something in the Shadows*, there is a reference to still another Dr. Mannerheim, though he never appears in the story. Prolific writers for the pulps and paperback originals often repeated character names out of haste and carelessness, but Packer never strikes the reader as a careless writer. She seems to know exactly what she is doing in using Dr. Mannerheims in three books, though what significance the name has for her is grist for a deeper study than this one.

The author's choice of character names is often intriguing. She would return to the title character's name in *The Damnation of Adam Blessing* (1960) for the main character in one of her M. E. Kerr novels, *The Son of Someone Famous* (1974). *Adam Blessing* drew another admiring review from Boucher, who wrote that Packer, "consistently the most sensitive and illuminating writer of paperback originals, is at her perceptive best" in "a full-scale and disquieting portrait of a psychopath" (*NYTBR*, February 1961, page 51).

In what may seem an extreme example of

drawing on real life, Packer uses her own real surname for the main character in *Something in the Shadows* (1961). Folklorist Joseph Meaker (yet another former University of Missouri student) has moved to a Pennsylvania farm with wife Maggie, who is employed in advertising in New York. Joseph is a confirmed, indeed extreme animal-lover, and when his cat Ishmael is run over by a doctor's Mercedes, Joseph begins to plot revenge. His plans take an odd course when he insists that he and Maggie befriend Dr. and Mrs. Hart, inviting them to dinner. The story is more like a standard suspense novel than most of Packer's, the reader suspecting that Meaker will murder but not knowing whom or how. The crime comes earlier in the book than usual, though still in the second half. Maggie's occupation provides the vehicle for some advertising parodies, notably a soft-sell cigarette commercial. ("Ladies and gentlemen, Pick cigarettes bring you three minutes of uninterrupted silence . . . . The public is tired of noisy commercials. They're irritating," page 20). Early in the novel, Joseph receives a letter from a Hungarian woman and former left-wing activist he knew at Missouri. The real-life origin of this character can be seen in the author's relationship with a Hungarian man, described in *Me Me Me Me Me*.

The writer Packer is most often compared to by reviewers is John O'Hara. That the influence is a real one is suggested by the O'Hara parody contained in *Something in the Shadows*, where one character imagines some O'Hara dialogue.

Indeed, Anthony Boucher, in reviewing Packer's next novel, *Intimate Victims* (1962), credits her "eye and ear for nice distinctions of culture and usage as acute as those of . . . O'Hara and Nancy Mitford" (*NYTBR*, 11 November, 1962, page 52). Reviewing the novel in tandem with Ross Macdonald's *The Zebra-Striped Hearse*, he finds in Packer "an almost

comparable amount of meat," high praise indeed
considering Boucher's view of Macdonald.   A closer
comparison in the crime/suspense field might be
Patricia Highsmith, as the relationship between main
characters Robert Bowser and Harvey Plangman has
something of a *Strangers on a Train* flavor.   For
once, a crime appears at the very beginning of the
book.   The treasurer of an investment firm, Bowser
has embezzled over $100,000, and he is planning his
imminent escape to Brazil when, through an
unfortunate stroke of fate, he inadvertently trades
jackets and wallets with Plangman in a service-
station restroom.   Obsessive social climber Plangman,
a pitiful collector of brand names and foreign phrases
who is one of Packer's most memorable characters,
finds the evidence of Bowser's plans and takes the
opportunity for an odd and elaborate blackmail plan:
Bowser must take Plangman's place as superintendent
of a boardinghouse near the University of Missouri,
while providing him evidence by mail on which clothes
to wear, brands to buy, and dishes to cook while
futilely courting a rich man's daughter.   Of course, the
scheme will culminate in murder, but again who will
murder whom is left to the end of the book.

Alone at Night (1963) is Vin Packer's last novel
for Gold Medal.   In fact, only two more novels under
the pseudonym would appear, one a hardcover.   Once
again, the setting is Cayuta, New York, in the Finger
Lakes.   This novel may represent Packer's closest
approach to a detective story, albeit an inverted one.
Buzzy Cloward went to prison for causing the death of
Carrie Burr, running her down while drunk and driving
her husband's car.   Now he returns to Cayuta, where
Carrie's husband Slater Burr has remarried.   The reader
soon comes to suspect that Cloward may not be guilty,
but any whodunit element is short-lived: Slater is the
person really responsible.   Awkward questions begin to
arise--how, for example, could the drunken Cloward
immediately figure out how to drive Burr's difficult and

unfamiliar Jaguar?--and the novel's suspense lies in
how (or whether) Burr will ultimately be found out.

The novel, though competent enough, lacks
Packer's usual zest. Boucher again reviewed a Packer
book in tandem with others, and again the company he
chose for her shows how highly she was regarded.
Alone at Night is bracketed with John D. MacDonald's
On the Run and Donald E. Westlake's *Killy* as examples
of sub-par performances by good writers. Boucher said
the "polish seems machine-made, without the exciting
creativity we have associated with these writers"
(*NYTBR*, 2 June, 1963, page 23).

The last Packer paperback original is better,
though still not in a class with the best books of the
fifties and early sixties. *The Hare in March* (Signet,
1966), like several of the novels from Gold Medal, is
given a cover blurb that emphasizes its trendiness: "A
shattering novel about the college boys and girls who
fly high on violence, sex, and L.S.D." As usual, it is
far less conventional and predictable than the blurb
might suggest. The first chapter suggests a traditional
mystery, as two Far Point, New York cops on patrol
discover a dead girl next to a spaced-out college boy
in a car at the local lover's lane. But the novel then
flashes back to the events leading up to the crime, in
a pattern like that in Packer's earliest books, albeit
somewhat more complex in plot. The scene is Far
Point College, where L.S.D. is used in a fraternity
hazing. Undersized Arnold Hagerman is a chilling
figure in the grand tradition of Packer psychopaths.
That Packer kept her finger on the pulse of the times
is indicated by her topical references--Vietnam protest
(still fairly early in 1966), Timothy Leary, camp, and a
couple of names that remain quite current today:
Ronald Reagan and Cher.

Following one more novel, the hardcover
astrology comedy *Don't Rely on Gemini* (Delacorte,

1969), the Packer byline was retired. In 1972, with the first M. E. Kerr book, the author almost immediately attained a firm place among the most celebrated authors of young adult "problem" novels. Few if any of the Kerrs could be classified as mystery and suspense, until the most recent one, *Fell* (1987), which is not only a mystery but introduces an element that could not be more foreign to the world of Vin Packer: a series detective!

M. E. Kerr's continued fame seems secure. But her alter ego Vin Packer is one of many authors of suspense fiction who are unjustly forgotten and deserve revival. She was a big seller in the fifties-- the back cover of *Dark Don't Catch Me* is already claiming 4-1/2 million copies sold--and Boucher considered her one of the best crime novelists of her day, regardless of format. A rereading of her novels today bears out his opinion. Though all her novels are of interest, the following seem to this reader the most deserving of rediscovery: *Come Destroy Me*, *Whisper His Sin*, *The Twisted Ones*, and *Something in the Shadows*.

Still, with all the recent reprinting activity in the mystery/suspense field, the Packer novels remain unavailable. Most of the major reference works-- *Encyclopedia of Mystery and Detection*, *Twentieth-Century Crime and Mystery Writers*, *1001 Midnights*, *A Catalogue of Crime*--omit her from coverage. It seems safe to predict, however, that this neglect won't continue. With the current surge of feminism in the crime-fiction world, no woman writer as outstanding as Vin Packer can be ignored for long.

Checklist: Vin Packer

Alone at Night (Gold Medal, 1963)
Come Destroy Me (Gold Medal, 1954)

The Damnation of Adam Blessing (Gold Medal, 1960)
Dark Don't Catch Me (Gold Medal, 1956)
Dark Intruder (Gold Medal, 1952)
Dinky Hooker Shoots Smack (as M. E. Kerr) (Harper, 1972) (hardcover)
Don't Rely on Gemini (Delacorte, 1969) (hardcover)
The Evil Friendship (Gold Medal, 1958)
Fell (as M. E. Kerr) (Harper, 1987) (hardcover)
5:45 to Suburbia (Gold Medal, 1958)
The Girl on the Bestseller List (Gold Medal, 1960)
The Hare in March (Signet, 1966)
Intimate Victims (Gold Medal, 1962)
Look Back on Love (Gold Medal, 1953)
Me Me Me Me Me (as M. E. Kerr) (Harper, 1983) (hardcover autobiography)
Shockproof Sydney Skate (as Marijane Meaker) (1972) (hardcover)
Something in the Shadows (Gold Medal, 1961)
The Son of Someone Famous (as M. E. Kerr) (Little, Brown, 1974) (hardcover)
Spring Fire (Gold Medal, 1952)
3 Day Terror (Gold Medal, 1952)
The Thrill Kids (Gold Medal, 1955)
The Twisted Ones (Gold Medal, 1959)
Whisper His Sin (Gold Medal, 1954)
The Young and the Violent (Gold Medal, 1956)

MARVIN H. ALBERT

by George Kelley

Marvin H. Albert is a prolific writer of mysteries, suspense fiction, westerns, and novelizations of screenplays. Although categorized as a journeyman writer by some critics, Albert manages to rise above the level of the Day Keenes and Orrie Hitts by the sophisticated plots and attention to detail in his paperback originals. After thirty-five years of writing, Albert is now producing a contemporary suspense series of high quality--the Stone Angel books--and finally getting the recognition that has escaped him.

In a career that has seen Albert producing fluff like novelizations of *The Pink Panther* and *Under the Yum Yum Tree*, and Executioner clones like the *Soldato!* series, achieving wide success in his sixties has to be particularly sweet.

Marvin Hubert Albert was born in Philadelphia in 1924. He served as a radio officer on Liberty ships in World War II. Before turning to writing full time, Albert served an apprenticeship as a copy writer for the Philadelphia *Record*, a researcher for *Look* magazine, and a television scriptwriter. Then, in the fifties, Albert turned to full-time writing; with the help of a few pseudonyms, he produced an average of five books per year for a decade.

The best of these early novels was published under his own name: *Lie Down With Lions* (Fawcett, 1955). Royan, once the Great White Hunter, has lost his courage: an African medicine man has cursed him. Royan, once strong and powerful, now has turned to alcohol to enable him to bear the curse put upon him. His wife, the sensual Jeanne, is confused and frightened by the change in her husband. Surrounded by jungle, she sees no escape for either of them.

George Murat, an engineer whom the African government has hired to clear the jungle for a construction operation, hopes to train natives to operate the heavy equipment and pay them minimally while pocketing the difference between the actual and budgeted wages. Murat meets Jeanne, senses her sexual frustration with Royan, and decides to seduce her.

But Murat goes further: he hires Royan to clear the jungle of the dangerous animals. Royan, given a sense of purpose, tries to escape the hold the liquor bottle has on him. He fails. Royan's native friend, N'jalda, finally tells Royan that the old medicine man is dead, that there is a new medicine man who can lift the curse put upon him. Royan seeks out the new medicine man and undergoes a hideous ceremony that banishes the curse. Royan is whole again.

Meanwhile, Murat has fallen in love with the sexy Jeanne, who remains more or less true to Royan. Murat sabotages Royan's weapons. When Royan and N'jalda head into the jungle to kill a rogue elephant, Royan's gun "jams" and N'jalda is stomped to death by the elephant.

Royan returns to Murat to get his revenge. He takes Murat deep into the jungles with a sabotaged weapon and leaves him there. The book ends,

When dawn crept into the jungle, it brought many sleeping animals awake. But not George Murat. He lay beside a marsh, staring unseeingly up at the boughs of an overhanging tree. The puncture wounds turned purple in his

distended throat, where the poisoned fangs of a
green mamba had stabbed him when he stumbled
against the dangling snake an hour before the
sun rose.

Albert's craftsmanship is clear in *Lie Down With
Lions.* The plot is complex, the characters are
carefully drawn, and the action is swift and
unpredictable. This novel shows many of Albert's
strengths that are lacking in other novels that seem
hurriedly written. This variable quality plagues
Albert's output: many of his works are first-rate, and
others are inferior because of two-dimensional
characters or a lack of attention to detail.

The Albert Conroy Books

"Albert Conroy" was Albert's favorite pseudonym.
He used it for his early series of crime novels for
Fawcett, used it again as "Al Conroy" for a successful
series of westerns in the sixties, and again in the
seventies when "Al Conroy" produced five volumes of
Executioner clones called the *Soldato!* series.

But the best of the Albert Conroy books is *The
Road's End* (Fawcett, 1952). Dan Ginger wakes up
without a memory. He's approached by a sexy young
girl named Carol Brill, whose father, Jim Brill, pulled
Ginger out of the river half-drowned. Carol nurses
Ginger back to health, but Ginger still can't remember
anything. Jim Brill is murdered, and Ginger vows to
avenge him. But Ginger is framed for murder and has
to solve the mystery of his own loss of memory in
order to clear himself.

The Road's End has a classic Gold Medal
situation: an innocent man is on the run and only
saves himself through the help of some nubile young
wench.

The Chiselers (Fawcett, 1953) introduces the theme of sexual obsession within the Mob. Jerry Stone and Morgan Diamond are partners on the police force. They have a set of tapes that could destroy the Mob if the Governor's Special State Investigator had their evidence. But the Mob knows this too and ambushes Jerry Stone outside his home. Stone dies, and Diamond doesn't know where Stone hid the tapes. Diamond refuses to cooperate with the Special Investigator, but does work with Stone's daughter to search for the tapes.

Diamond also seeks to avenge Stone's murder more personally by bringing down the men who killed him. But in his investigation, Diamond falls for Carmen, a sexy singer who wants to see her mobster lover, Wabash, killed so that she can pursue a Hollywood career. Carmen uses Diamond to kill Wabash but dies in her own twisted plot.

Albert isn't afraid of downbeat endings like the one in *The Chiselers*. He isn't afraid to leave his heroes hurt and bleeding at the book's end. The Albert Conroy books work within the Gold Medal formula, but Albert doesn't hesitate to take chances and tinker with the formula for maximum suspense.

If there is a flaw in these early books, it is too much plot: *The Chiselers* also has a subplot in which Wabash is trying to bring down gang boss Alzamora's empire. That's a lot of action for a 160-page book; action that the slightness of the characters sometimes fails to carry off.

Three more outstanding Albert Conroy books are *Nice Guys Finish Dead* (Fawcett, 1957), *Murder in Room 13* (Fawcett, 1958), and *The Mob Says Murder* (Fawcett, 1958).

Murder in Room 13 opens with a tough scene: Steve Fusario, a trucker who gets picked up by a beautiful but scared woman named Maude Sarrow, is being worked over by a team of police interrogators who are convinced he murdered Maude. Morgan, a brutal police detective, vows he'll fry Fusario. When a mysterious man with a .45 arranges Fusario's escape, Steve has to avoid the police and the murderer in order to clear himself from an airtight frame. *Murder in Room 13* displays Albert's strength at headlong, breathless, first-person action narrative.

The Mob Says Murder features a savvy, rock-hard convict named Edward Driscoll. The mob breaks him out of prison, but in return they want Driscoll to assassinate the crime-busting Governor. The book features a hulking killer, Arno, who has to keep control of Driscoll until the assassination plot can come together. But Driscoll figures the mob intends to use him for a fall guy and comes up with his own tricky plot to bring down gang boss Bruno Hauser. The fiery conclusion contains a typical Albert plot twister.

The Al Conroy books are a big step down in class: they were written to take advantage of the Mafia craze in the early seventies and cloned the bestselling formula of the Executioner, Butcher, and Penetrator men's action series.

Soldato! (Lancer, 1972) introduces Johnny Morini, a soldier in the New York Mafia. The old Italian who raised Johnny had gotten behind in his payments to the Mafia shylocks. While Johnny was out of town, some Mafia thugs gang raped the old Italian's daughter to teach him a lesson about delayed payments. The daughter committed suicide, and the old Italian was blown away the next day attempting to kill Johnny's Mafia boss to avenge his daughter. Clearly, melodrama is the order of the day in the *Soldato!* books.

With the two closest people to him dead, Johnny vows vengeance and brings down one of the most powerful Mafia families in New York. But, with his death promised by an open Mafia contract, Johnny turns to the Department of Justice as a protected witness. He damages the Mafia some more, and in return, Johnny is set up with a new identity. A couple years pass, and Johnny thinks he's safe. He marries, but the Mafia never forgets. They hunt him down and Johnny is forced to kill the hitmen. Johnny's pregnant wife miscarries, realizes she doesn't want to be married to a secret killer, and leaves Johnny. Johnny figures the only safe place for him is on the road.

The second book, *Death Grit!* (Lancer, 1972), introduces some stability of plotting with dying millionaire Carmine Pannunzio and his agent, Riley, convincing Johnny the only way to bring down the Mafia is a series of infiltrating raids by an insider. Johnny agrees and, with Pannunzio's funding, takes on Max Vigilante's Mafia empire in Philly. The rest of the book is typical action, murder, and gunplay. Satisfying, though not very sophisticated.

Book three, *Blood Run* (Lancer, 1973), has Johnny taking on the Mafia in Florida; book four has Johnny breaking up the mob in New Orleans. The formula stays fairly standard, and the action has the brutality desired by readers of this violent genre. But either Albert tired of this hackwork after five books, or the market declined, or Lancer's poor financial position caused the series to end after the fifth book.

The Nick Quarry Books

The Nick Quarry books present a hardboiled private eye in a series of mediocre mystery novels. *The Hoods Came Calling* (Fawcett, 1958) introduces

Jake Barrow, a Chicago private eye who comes to New York City to buy out a retiring colleague and set up a new practice in the Big Apple.

Jake meets his ex-wife Carla at a party and demands the money she took out of their joint account so he can buy the detective agency. They have a public fight, and Jake leaves the party. The next day, Carla is found dead and Jake is the prime suspect. Jake has to find the killers before the police find him.

The action is swift, the writing is solid, and the plotting is a step above the usual Gold Medal original. But the book lacks the impact of most hard-boiled detective series of the day. Jake is too cerebral for the stereotypical tough-guy private eye, who's supposed to think with his fists and his .45.

In *Trail of a Tramp* (Fawcett, 1958), Jake has his detective agency, and one of his first cases comes from a mysterious little man who hires Jake to find his "daughter," Julia Hiller. Jake discovers the woman was a stripper and a prostitute. Other people are looking for her, too, so Jake has to kick into high gear to solve the mystery and find the girl before she ends up a corpse. Albert does a nice job in *Trail of a Tramp* showing the details of a missing person investigation. The book's conclusion contains a nifty surprise with Julia Hiller's identity.

In *The Girl With No Place to Hide* (Fawcett, 1959), echoes of *Murder in Room 13* abound. Jake Barrow saves a frightened girl named Angela Hart from a beating, and the girl pleads with him to take her to his apartment. Jake is called away, and when he returns, the body of Angela Hart is waiting for him on his apartment floor. The search for the dead girl's killer leads Jake to a woman photographer who is later murdered, the dark side of the fashion

industry, and the professional fixing of heavyweight
fights. *The Girl With No Place to Hide* is the
strongest of the Jake Barrow books.

No Chance in Hell (Fawcett, 1960) features Nina
Cloud, a beautiful American Indian girl stalked by
killers. Jake has to save her and her father, John
Cloud, from professional killer Ben Hanks. The death
stalk in New Mexico is the book's highlight.

In the last Jake Barrow book, *Some Die Hard*
(Fawcett, 1961), Jake is under a death sentence by
the biggest gangster in New York City, Frank Leca.
Leca's son is dead, and Frank blames Jake Barrow for
the murder. The only way Jake can stay alive is to
prove his innocence--and give Leca the real murderer.
Again, the plot is clever and the action swift, but the
characters remain the consistency of cardboard. The
variability of the quality of the Jake Barrow books
leads to the series' mediocrity. The best book is *The
Girl With No Place to Hide*, but the other volumes are
far from that standard.

The other two Nick Quarry titles, *The Don Is
Dead* (Fawcett, 1972) and *The Vendetta* (Fawcett,
1972), are hackwork written quickly to take advantage
of *The Godfather* craze that accompanied Mario Puzo's
novel--also published by Fawcett in paperback--and the
Francis Ford Coppola hit movie. They are a bit better
than the *Soldato!* series, but not much.

The Anthony Rome Books

The Anthony Rome books contain some of
Albert's best writing. *Miami Mayhem* (Pocket Books,
1960) introduces Tony Rome, a Miami cop turned
private who's a compulsive gambler. Rome's father,
also on the Miami police force, exposed the crooked
dealings of a powerful politician. In retaliation,

information about Rome's father's embarrassing activities to raise money for his dying wife was released to the press. Rome's father committed suicide, and Tony Rome quit the force. Now Rome lives on a boat, *Straight Pass*, he won in a card game--shades of Travis McGee--and solves cases to get the money for another run at breaking the bank at Las Vegas.

In *Miami Mayhem*, Rome's former partner is murdered and Rome has to work fast to avoid a murder charge. *Miami Mayhem* and the next book in the series, *The Lady in Cement* (Pocket Books, 1961), were made into movies starring Frank Sinatra as Rome. When *Miami Mayhem* was filmed as *Tony Rome*, the novel was rereleased under that title (Dell, 1967) by Marvin H. Albert.

The Lady in Cement is better than *Miami Mayhem*, though much the inferior movie. Tony Rome goes skindiving and finds the nude body of a girl embedded in a block of cement. The search for the killers leads Rome to "retired" gangster Al Mungo. Mungo warns Rome off the case; later, Rome is framed for another murder which leads to the book's most exciting scenes: Rome avoiding a police dragnet of Miami Beach.

But the best Tony Rome book is the last one: *My Kind of Game* (Dell, 1962). Rome's good friend, Lou Kovac, was on a case in a grim Florida town called Coffin City when he was viciously attacked and methodically beaten. Rome vows revenge, travels to Coffin City, and picks up the case. Rome finds out that Hugh Tallant runs the town from his private gambling club, the Algiers Club. Tallant controls the police through its chief, Hollis Cobb. But there's going to be an election at the end of the month and Serena Ferguson, editor of the Coffin City *Clarion*, and a group of reformers have made Tallant and Cobb very

nervous. After Rome is shot in an ambush, he awakes
at Tallant's club.   Tallant tells Rome he and Cobb are
the only forces standing in the way of a mob takeover
of Coffin City--and instead of saving the city, the
reformers would doom it if they win the election.
When reform candidate Gil Hurley is found murdered,
Rome has to solve two mysteries: who killed Gil Hurley
and where was Hurley's old girlfriend, Carol Branco,
the key to the entire case? *My Kind of Game* is one
of Marvin H. Albert's very best books. And the Tony
Rome series contains some of Albert's best work.

The Ian MacAlister Books

        Alistair MacLean was in his twilight, but Fawcett
books, publisher of MacLean's books in paperback,
decided to clone his high adventure series with another
high adventure series by "Ian MacAlister," whose books
would sit right next to MacLean's on the bookstore
shelves.

        Albert's four Ian MacAlister books are of
varying quality. The first, *Skylark Mission* (Fawcett,
1973), is clearly the worst. It concerns a group of
refugees trying to move through Japanese-held islands
to the safety of New Zealand. They are captured, but
one of the sailors escapes and reaches New Zealand.
There, the impossible Skylark Mission is hatched: two
military men, the sailor, and a drunken pilot with a
seaplane, the Skylark, will return to the Japanese-held
island and free the prisoners.

        The plot lacks realism and Albert seems
uncomfortable with the setting. The island never
becomes tangible, and the characters are totally
shallow. The only remarkable aspect of the book is
Albert's willingness to sacrifice one of the lead
characters at the book's conclusion. Yet the next
book, *Driscoll's Diamonds* (Fawcett, 1973), is top-flight

high adventure. Driscoll is a mercenary who's found by an Israeli patrol; at first, they thought he was dead, but on closer inspection, they found him dehydrated and near death. After a hospital stay, Driscoll recovered and fell in love with a beautiful Israeli nurse, Shana.

Then, Shana is kidnapped by Royan--yes, the character from Albert's very good early book *Lie Down With Lions* returns as the leader of a band of mercenaries who accuse Driscoll of stealing a fortune in diamonds. They will kill Shana unless Driscoll recovers them.

The rest of the book recounts the adventures of the mercenary band taking on the desert elements and threats of the savage bands of terrorists to gain the diamonds. The conclusion, with its bittersweet ending featuring Royan's last heroic act, is particularly moving. *Driscoll's Diamonds* is equal to the best of Alistair MacLean. Albert clearly is having fun in this book by recycling characters from other books: Driscoll from *The Mob Says Murder*, the "Albert Conroy" classic, also reappears.

Strike Force 7 (Fawcett, 1974) doesn't quite equal the pleasures of *Driscoll's Diamonds* but does deliver an exciting adventure. Arab terrorists in Morocco plan to kidnap U.S. Senator Bishop when he lands at his estate there. But Bishop is delayed, and the terrorists kidnap Bishop's wife and stepdaughter and threaten to kill them unless hundreds of jailed terrorists are released.

Bishop hires a band of seven unlikely mercenaries to rescue his wife and stepdaughter. The mercenaries track the terrorists down in the savage Atlas mountains. The action is swift, and the conclusion powerful. *Strike Force 7* is solid entertainment.

Albert returns to the Middle East with the last
Ian MacAlister book, *Valley of the Assassins* (Fawcett,
1975).   Albert certainly has captured the feeling of the
blazing, dangerous deserts of the Middle East.   Captain
Eric Larson comes into possession of a map leading to
the fabulous treasures contained in the coffin of
Hasan-i-Sabbah, leader of the hundreds-of-years-old
Order of the Assassins.   The map is told in a series of
riddles Larson must solve, but when he does, he takes
a rag-tag band into the desert to the hiding place:
Darra, the sexy Kurd terrorist Larson loves; Hammad,
the secret police chief who is risking his career on
this treasure hunt; Slasko, a gun-runner and thug;
Jamil, Darra's fellow terrorist; and Jim Church, an oil
expert who can give them access to the lands where
the treasure is hidden.

The journey is exciting: the band is stalked both
by Bedouin raiders and the mysterious members of the
Order of the Assassins.   The conclusion, in typical
Albert style, is both exciting and bittersweet.   *Valley
of the Assassins* is another top-notch adventure novel.

All the Ian MacAlister books are highly
recommended, with the exception of the disappointing
first one, *Skylark Mission*.

The Big Books

With the publication of *The Gargoyle Conspiracy*
(Doubleday, 1975), Albert entered a decade in which he
wrote long, involved, sometimes ponderous hardcover
suspense novels.   The books benefited from the
background and research Albert did on the Middle
East for the Ian MacAlister books.

In *The Gargoyle Conspiracy*, Ahmed Bel Jahra--a
Moroccan terrorist based on Bel Zaara, the Moroccan

terrorist in *Strike Force 7*--plans to assassinate the U.S. Secretary of State and King Hussein of Jordan during a birthday party for an aging artist in southern France.

On Bel Jahra's trail are two men: George Shansky, an ex-CIA agent, and Simon Hunter, member of an American anti-terrorism group. Together, they track Bel Jahra across Europe until the final spectacular shoot-out. *The Gargoyle Conspiracy* ranks with the best of the Ian MacAlister high adventure books.

The Dark Goddess (Doubleday, 1978) is important because it introduces Peter Sawyer, who will later come to star in the Stone Angel series. Nobel Prize-winning historian and presidential advisor Alexander Rhalles finds his wife has been kidnapped by the KGB. They give Rhalles a choice: turn over top-secret transcripts of his meetings with the President or they'll brutally murder his wife, Moira.

Rhalles feels his only option is to contact Moira's former lover, Peter Sawyer, who has unique talents in the area of industrial espionage. *The Dark Goddess* has a twisting plot and frantic action. Albert develops the character of Peter Sawyer into his best realized creation.

The Medusa Complex (Arbor, 1981) is much less successful. The Medusa is a super assassin, a woman of beauty and cunning who proves irresistible to her victims. Tangled in this plot is a Soviet mole who acts as a leading industrialist but secretly acquires control of multinational companies. The action gets tedious, and the characters never come alive.

Hidden Lives (Delacorte, 1981) suffers from some of the same problems: a ponderous plot where a young man, Nicholas Grayle, a talented painter in Paris, flees

France because of a murder charge, joins the Foreign
Legion, takes up with a Berber tribe in Morocco, then
returns to France just as the Germans are invading.
The plot never jells, and with exception of the desert
scenes, the settings just don't ring true.

In *Operation Lila* (Arbor, 1983), Albert returns
to a setting he hasn't had much success with in the
past: World War II.   France has fallen to the
Germans, and they plan to capture the French fleet at
Toulon.   British intelligence has proof of the
Germans' plans, but the skeptical French admirals
won't believe it until they see it.   Jonas Ruyter, a
savvy British intelligence agent, is selected to get the
proof to the French.   The excitement builds as Ruyter
races across France with the Gestapo, the SS, and
traitorous Frenchmen chasing him.   *Operation Lila*
succeeds best when Albert's French settings come
alive with unusual realism.

But the decade of Albert's big books was
ultimately disappointing.   *The Gargoyle Conspiracy* and
The Dark Goddess are the best of the lot, but too
often the long books lost much of their impact
because of ponderous subplots and more ponderous
characters.

Triumph at Last: The Stone Angel Books

With *Stone Angel* (Fawcett, 1986), Albert finally
achieves the success he's flirted with over his long
career.   Peter Sawyer narrates the books in a
sophisticated style, and Albert captures the settings in
France beautifully.   Sawyer is a hybrid: son of an
American pilot shot down over France in World War II
and a mother who achieved fame as a French
resistance fighter.   Sawyer grew up being raised by his
grandparents in Chicago, but spending summers with
his brilliant, scholarly mother in France.   His mother

named him Pierre-Ange--Peter in English, Stone Angel
in French.

After a successful career as an investigator in
America, Sawyer leaves the States to pursue a career
in France as an escape from some unpleasant activities
for which Washington still holds a grudge against him.

In the first book, Sawyer is hired by a wealthy
American couple to find their daughter, a spoiled
teenager who's supposed to be taking classes in Paris.
Sawyer discovers the daughter, Sarah Byrnes, has taken
up with a young man who may be a terrorist. Sawyer
locates Sarah leaving the young man's apartment, is
attacked by other terrorists, and is left for dead. The
plot is satisfactorily complex as Sawyer follows the
clues that lead back to World War II and the
aristocratic Lemaire family, whose Champagne empire
may be about to fall.

The second book in the series, *Back in the Real
World* (Fawcett, 1986), builds on the success of the
first. When Sawyer drops by his friend Frank
Crowley's house and finds the murdered bodies of
Frank's wife and another private detective, he gets
embroiled in a complex plot dealing with the French
fashion industry and a rogue French intelligence agent
who is heavily into blackmail. Only Sawyer can solve
the puzzle of the murders before Frank Crowley is
condemned to death.

Get Off at Babylon (Fawcett, 1987) is the most
unconventional Peter Sawyer thriller. Former Grand
Prix champion racer Egon Mulhausser hires Sawyer to
find his daughter, Odile Garnier. Sawyer discovers
Odile is a drug addict who's ripped off a drug
shipment belonging to crime boss Fulvio Callega.
Callega puts out a contract on Odile, and Sawyer is in
a desperate race against time to find Odile before
someone blows her away. The search takes Sawyer

into the underground caverns beneath Paris to a unique, eerie world few know exists. Sawyer's search is filled with tension, and his plan to save Odile from Callega's contract is particularly well done.

Albert's latest, longest, and best Stone Angel book is *Long Teeth* (Fawcett, 1987). Sawyer's hired to deliver the ransom for the wife of industrialist Karl Malo. But with the exchange, Sawyer gets deeper into the Malo family's problems as he investigates Malo's brilliant son, Alexandre, his secretive daughter, Claudette, and his too-good-to-be-true son-in-law, Jean-Noel. Together with the appearance of ex-CIA agent, Johnny Duncan, Sawyer has his hands full sorting out the plots and counterplots surrounding Karl Malo's empire.

Albert displays a depth in *Long Teeth*, with careful development of character and complex plotting. The book never veers into the ponderousness of some of his longer works, but takes a detailed look at the international kidnapping situation and the power politics of a powerful family. *Long Teeth* is a tour-de-force.

The Stone Angel series is the best, most consistent writing Marvin H. Albert has done in a forty-year career. The series shows the professionalism Albert has learned and earned over that time. With these books, Albert is at the top of his form.

Checklist: Marvin H. Albert

Back in the Real World (Gold Medal, 1986)
Blood Run (as Al Conroy) (Lancer, 1973)
The Chiselers (as Albert Conroy) (Gold Medal, 1953)
The Dark Goddess (Doubleday, 1978) (hardcover)
Death Grip! (as Al Conroy) (Lancer, 1972)

The Don Is Dead (as Nick Quarry) (Gold Medal, 1972)
Driscoll's Diamonds (as Ian MacAlister) (Gold Medal, 1973)
The Gargoyle Conspiracy (Doubleday, 1975) (hardcover)
Get Off at Babylon (Gold Medal, 1987)
The Girl With No Place to Hide (as Nick Quarry) (Gold Medal, 1959)
Hidden Lives (Delacorte, 1981) (hardcover)
The Hoods Came Calling (as Nick Quarry) (Gold Medal, 1958)
The Lady in Cement (as Anthony Rome) (Pocket, 1961)
Lie Down with Lions (Gold Medal, 1955)
Long Teeth (Gold Medal, 1987)
The Medusa Complex (Arbor, 1981) (hardcover)
Miami Mayhem (as Anthony Rome) (Pocket, 1960)
The Mob Says Murder (as Albert Conroy) (Gold Medal, 1958)
Murder in Room 13 (as Albert Conroy) (Gold Medal, 1957)
My Kind of Game (as Anthony Rome) (Dell, 1962)
Nice Guys Finish Dead (as Albert Conroy) (Gold Medal, 1957)
No Chance in Hell (as Nick Quarry) (Gold Medal, 1957)
Operation Lila (Arbor, 1983) (hardcover)
The Pink Panther (Bantam, 1964) (novelization)
The Road's End (as Albert Conroy) (Gold Medal, 1952)
Skylark Mission (as Ian MacAlister) (Gold Medal, 1973)
Soldato! (as Al Conroy) (Lancer, 1972)
Some Die Hard (as Nick Quarry) (Gold Medal, 1961)
Stone Angel (Gold Medal, 1986)
Strike Force 7 (as Ian MacAlister) (Gold Medal, 1974)
Trail of a Tramp (as Nick Quarry) (Gold Medal, 1958)
Under the Yum Yum Tree (Dell, 1963) (novelization)
Valley of the Assassins (as Ian MacAlister) (Gold

Medal, 1975)
The Vendetta (as Nick Quarry) (Gold Medal, 1972)

FIFTEEN IMPRESSIONS OF CHARLES WILLIAMS

by Ed Gorman

1

"He was a hard luck kind of guy. He was much better than many writers who really made it. Not that he'd ever tell you, of course. He was genuinely modest, maybe even a little down on what he wrote. You could never be sure if he thought what he did was quite respectable. He was, after all, writing paperback originals and this was still the 1950s."

This is his agent Don Congdon talking on a late New York afternoon when autumn is giving bitter birth to winter.

2

When she was through being sick, I wet a wash cloth at the basin and bathed her face while she leaned weakly against the bathroom wall with her eyes closed. She didn't open them until she was back on the bed. She took one long look at me and said, 'Oh, good God!' and closed them again. She made a feeble attempt to pull her skirt down. I straightened it for her, and she lay still. I went out in the living room and lighted a cigarette. I could handle her all right, but if the police came by again and noticed those garage doors were unlocked, I was dead. It would be at least three more hours before it was dark.

This is from *Man On The Run*, November, 1958, and in many respects the seminal Gold Medal Original, involving as it does, a) a falsely accused man trying to elude police, b) a lonely woman as desperate in her way as the man on the run, c) enough atmospherics (night, rain, fog) to enshroud a hundred *films noir*. In its simple, yearning, painful way, it is one of the best thrillers of its era. It has now been out of print for thirty years.

3

According to *Twentieth Century Crime and Mystery Writers* (second edition), Charles Williams was born in San Angelo, Texas on August 13, 1909; was educated at Brownsville High School, Texas (only through the tenth grade), served with the United States Merchant Marine, married Lasca Foster in 1939, had one daughter, and died in 1975.

What it doesn't tell us is how he died. On that same late New York afternoon, his agent Congdon described the details, and it's now a month and a half later and I can't forget those details. Not at all.

4

In an exceptional essay on Williams, critic Geoffrey O'Brien noted: "Charles Williams is at face value the epitome of a macho adventure writer. His heros are characteristically pre-occupied with hunting (*Hill Girl*), fishing (*River Girl*; *Go Home, Stranger*; *Girl Out Back*), athletics (*The Big Bite*; *A Touch of Death*), and, above all, sailing (*Scorpion Reef*; *Sailcloth Shroud*; *Dead Calm*)."

Then O'Brien neatly goes on to point out that

while the trappings of the book may seem standard blue collar--especially the early "hill" books--their real theme is "the hero's discovery that he knows nothing about women."

It is Williams' women we remember most, from the innocent girl in *Hell Hath No Fury*, to the sullen and deadly Cathy Dunbar in *Nothing in Her Way*, and the enigmatic Mrs. Langston in *Talk of the Town*.

No other power--not in Williams' world anyway--can match women's to redeem or destroy.

5

"It's actually kind of a funny story, how I met Charlie. In those days--this is back in the late 40s--I was an editor at Simon and Schuster and his first novel came in over the transom; the writing was exceptionally good for a new writer but the plot was deemed by me and several others to be too commercial for hardcovers of that day, so the manuscript was returned to Charlie.

"Later, I left Simon and Schuster and joined the Harold Matson Company as an agent. I wrote a few writers whose work I had seen at Simon and Schuster to see if they would let me handle their work. Charlie sent me the same novel and I offered it to some other hardcover publishers, and it was turned down.

"Charlie suggested I throw it away, but I didn't. I put the manuscript on the shelf and a year or so later when Fawcett started their line of paperback originals which they called Gold Medals, I remembered Charlie's work, sent it over to them, and they bought it immediately. I had difficulty reaching Charlie to give him the good news, but finally did. The novel, which was entitled *Hill Girl*, went on to sell two and a half million copies."

6

The French, more than any other people, love the suspense story. Gallimard, in its famous mystery/suspense series *Serie Noire*, has kept most of Charlie's novels in print for many years. People such as Truffaut were interested in his novels and Jeanne Moreau and Belmondo starred in *Nothing in Her Way*, the first novel to be filmed.

"Hollywood was never as interested," says Congdon, "and the early paperback novels usually elicited contempt from most of the people out there, who thought they were 'pulp.'

"However, one of his novels, *The Wrong Venus*, did sell to Universal and Charlie was hired to write the screenplay. He was disgusted with that experience because the screenplay was pretty much rewritten for James Garner. He worked on a second screenplay of someone else's work, but it also turned out to be a poor film."

7

Not that during this period--'57-'58--the book career is moving along so marvelously either.

For some reason, the whole original paperback response to the suspense novel began to subside, and Charlie's audience shrank along with it. Sales simply weren't as big as they had been, with the exception of those writers who decided to do their suspense mysteries around a single detective or lead character, as John D. MacDonald did. Charlie was asked to do this, but he said it would bore him silly writing about the same guy each time.

Congdon and Williams went to Dell and Knox Burger with the idea that Charlie's work ought to be in hardcover. Knox was willing to go along with a first hardcover printing if they could find a publisher and work out the appropriate arrangements. This was done with several of his novels, the first, *Scorpion Reef*, being at Macmillan.

They even talked to him about writing a series. Williams felt about series fiction much as he did about Hollywood.

Italy, Spain and France--there Charlie is hot hot hot.

In the States, to Congdon, he says: "Sometimes I wouldn't mind giving it all up and just being a beach bum."

8

Charles Williams wrote in a definitive way about used car lots, drive-up restaurants, motels, gun shops, loafing, sex with women you don't trust, inhaling cigarettes on chilly mornings, people who just look stupid, loneliness, inadequacy, fear, acceptance and dread.

He wrote a great deal about dread.

9

So Orson Welles, through this lawyer he had, buys this book of Charlie's and says he's going to make it into a film. Now Charlie had had several films made, but the idea was that Welles' standing and taste would be sufficient to expect that the film would be good. High hopes. Well, it did get made, but not all of it.

Jeanne Moreau, who was in the film, she said she'd seen early rushes and thought the film was a good one, but that Orson still wanted to tinker with it. And you heard on the talk shows from time to time about how more parts of it are getting made and soon now it will be done. But it was never released.

10

You see why I wake up this way? It's a dream I have.

I'm sitting there in the car watching her come out of that last bank and swing toward me across the sidewalk in the sun with the coppery hair shining and that tantalizing smile of Suzie's on her face and all that unhampered Suzie running loose inside that summer dress, seeing her and thinking that in only a few minutes we'll be in the apartment with the blinds drawn, in the semigloom, with a small overnight bag open on the floor beside the bed with $120,000 in fat bundles of currency inside it and maybe one nylon stocking, a sheer nylon, dropped by someone who didn't care where it fell . . .

And then in this dream she waves three fingers of her left hand and saunters on down the street, past me, and she's gone, and I'm trapped in a car in traffic at high noon in the middle of a city of 400,000, where two hundred cops are just waiting for me to step out on the street so they can spot me. I wake up.

Scream?

Who wouldn't.

--A Touch of Death

11

In the early 1970s, his wife died of cancer. Charles Williams bought some land up on the border between California and Oregon and went there to live in a trailer. Alone.

"He'd call and he'd sound depressed," Congdon says, "and I'd say, 'Charlie, you sound really depressed, why don't you get out of there?'

"It rained all that winter and he didn't write much, couldn't get a new book going. Charlie felt that once decent weather came along, living close to the river where he could fish, that things would work out. But there were complications about building a house, so he sold the property and moved down to Los Angeles."

12

"Charlie worked on some screenplay with Nona Tyson, a friend, who was Steven Spielberg's assistant and secretary. Her support seemed to help Charlie start writing again. He finished *Man on a Leash* and things looked as if they were going to be fine after all."

13

Charlie had one child, a daughter named Alison, and Williams was proud of her because she was especially bright.

14

"It was very strange," Congdon says. "So cold and purposeful. One morning I'm sitting in my office and I get a letter from Charlie and it says that by the time I read this, he'll have killed himself, which is exactly what he did.

"I couldn't tell you why, not for sure, and I would rather not speculate on it.

"Charlie was a smooth and polished writer, and he worked so hard on his books. He deserved more attention to his work in the United States, particularly in the film studios. He had the misfortune of writing suspense novels at a time when the public didn't seem to have as much interest in the genre."

15

Charles Williams wrote in a definitive way about pretty women, the way dust motes tumble in the sunlight, how pink a kitten's tongue is, how booze tastes when you're angry, how booze tastes when you're sad and how booze tastes when you're alone in the woods and not thinking of anything special at all.

But mostly, Charles Williams wrote in a definitive way about all of us, brothers and sisters, fathers and sons, mothers and daughters, people unremarkable in any overt way, just fearful people finally, floating on daydreams and obstinate hope before the final darkness.

Checklist: Charles Williams

The Big Bite (Dell, 1956)
Dead Calm (Viking, 1963) (hardcover)
Girl Out Back (Dell, 1958)
Go Home, Stranger (Gold Medal, 1954)
Hell Hath No Fury (Gold Medal, 1951)
Hill Girl (Gold Medal, 1951)
Man on a Leash (Putnam, 1973) (hardcover)
Man on the Run (Gold Medal, 1958)
Nothing in Her Way (Gold Medal, 1953)
River Girl (Gold Medal, 1951)
The Sailcloth Shroud (Viking, 1960) (hardcover)
Scorpion Reef (Macmillan, 1955) (hardcover)
Talk of the Town (Dell, 1958)
A Touch of Death (Gold Medal, 1954)

DONALD HAMILTON: THE WRITING CREW

by Loren D. Estleman

The argument took place during a university art class, and although it was the early seventies, our differences had nothing to do with Watergate or Vietnam or marijuana. My opponent was holding forth on the superiority of Ian Fleming's James Bond to all other spies in fiction, and I was steadfastly arguing in favor of Donald Hamilton's Matt Helm.

"Matt Helm?" he sneered. "You mean that slapstick letch in Dean Martin movies?"

Here was where I had him; for while my opposite number was familiar with only a handful of the Fleming titles and those dismal tongue-in-cheek films starring Martin as an amiable, girl-chasing imitation of the Bond of Hollywood, who was *himself* a pale shadow of Fleming's grim protagonist, I had read the entire output of both their creators.

"No," said I. "I mean that paid assassin for an unnamed U.S. Government agency, who although he prefers knives to guns, would cheerfully shoot to death an unarmed enemy, if those are his instructions or if the enemy is in his way, and preferably from behind, because it's plain damn foolishness to offer yourself as a target unless it's necessary. I mean a spy you can believe in, not a scar-faced boor who drives a '34 Bentley, smokes Players cigarettes, wears Sea Island shirts, and knows how to pronounce *chemin-de-fer*. A spy for today rather than some retired British civil servant's wet-dream for the postwar generation."

Well, that's how I'd have answered him if I'd been that articulate. I fancy I held my own. Bond, I argued, was a wimp: Hadn't he, in "The Living Daylights," against all orders, refused to kill a sniper during an attempted assassination, simply because she was a woman? On the other hand, Helm, toward the close of *Death of a Citizen*, his first adventure-- published two years before "The Living Daylights"-- went to work on a female enemy agent with a knife in the bathroom of his comfortable home, killing her in the process of interrogation, both because the information was crucial and because she'd threatened to do as much or worse to his wife and three children if he refused to cooperate with her. True, it cost him his marriage when his wife found out what a savage character she'd been hooked up with all those years; but he'd gotten the information.

I don't remember how the argument ended. I suspect my opponent went away unconvinced that Helm's incarnadine capers were any closer to the truth than Bond's gadgets and ridiculous .25 Beretta. This was before Congress and the press exposed the CIA's involvement in organized crime, the overthrow of the Chilean government, and the delivery of a box of poisoned cigars to Fidel Castro. Even at that time, in the midst of the partisan struggle between Nixon's wiretaps and Senator Ervin's eyebrows, Hamilton's tales of slaughter on behalf of democracy seemed farfetched; now they read like documentaries. Imagine, then, the reaction when the series debuted in 1960, the year John F. Kennedy was elected President. Small wonder that JFK, who kept company with Marilyn Monroe and believed that many of the nation's ills could be cured if everyone took fifty-mile hikes, preferred James Bond.

This is not to assert that Hamilton introduced realism to espionage fiction; Graham Greene and Somerset Maugham can claim dual credit for that. Nor may it be said that he invented the concept of the murderous protagonist; for that, one must go back before the First World War to those fantastically successful pulps featuring the archcriminal Fantomas. Put simply, the Matt Helm books represent the longest-running and most popular series narrated by an unregenerate killer presented as sympathetic.

When first we meet him, Helm is 36, living in Santa Fe with his wife and three children on his earnings as a professional photographer and author of westerns. (Hamilton, who began his career writing grimly realistic westerns and lives contentedly in Santa Fe, New Mexico, to this day, is being autobiographical here.) Neither Helm's wife Beth nor their children are aware of his violent past as a field agent during World War II. The peace of their home is shattered when a woman known only as Tina appears Banquo-like at a party at the Helms' to remind him of the danger and love they shared fifteen years before. Ere long the retired operative is caught up in the treacherous maelstrom of war in his own backyard. From violence he came, and by trail's end--having had to learn all over again that no one is to be trusted, least of all those closest to him--to violence, like Jack Schaefer's Shane, he must return. A spy is reborn and, as the book's title indicates, a citizen dies.

It was not meant to be thus. Hamilton has said that he planned to write an antiheroic story whose protagonist, having been plucked from a peaceful existence, performs his enforced duty, then returns to his happy *ennui*, vowing never again to stray onto forbidden ground. Firmly in the antiheroic vein, he christened his character George Helm. A frantic telephone call from his agent complaining that the name lacked pizzazz forced Hamilton to change it on the spot, with the help of a convenient Bible, to Matthew. Similarly, eleventh-hour Muses compelled Margaret Mitchell to change the designation of *Gone*

With the Wind's heroine from Pansy to Scarlett, and
Sir Arthur Conan Doyle to ditch Sherrinford for
Sherlock. The emendation was fortuitous, for it is
difficult to imagine a 24-volume (at last count) series
about a spy named George, not to mention a number of
inexplicably popular films featuring Dean Martin, or a
quite understandably short-lived television series
starring the abysmal Tony Franciosa.

Hamilton's readers know his hero equally well as
Eric, the code name by which he is recognized in the
field and in the office of the enigmatic Mac, director
of the small, tightly-knit organization of exterminators
for which Helm works--alternately referred to as "the
wrecking crew," "murderers' row," and "M" (for murder;
not to be confused with James Bond's boss). No crusty
avuncular M, Mac is a coldly reasoning automaton who
dispatches his angels of death to the four corners of
the world while he sits with graying hair and black
eyebrows at his desk with his back to a bright window,
monitoring their movements by telephone and gently
correcting their English. Sentiment plays no part in
his thinking process; at the height of the airplane-
hijack scare he muses that if the United States Air
Force were to shoot just two pirated craft out of the
air regardless of how many innocents were abroad, the
threat would cease, and as late as *The Demolishers*
(1987), he informs Helm, who has just lost his older
son to a terrorist bombing shortly after handing in his
resignation, that he would not have hesitated to
arrange the killing himself if he'd thought it would
return his most reliable agent to the fold. To his
arguable credit, if circumstances warranted Mac would
do the same with his own daughter--and very nearly
does in *The Intriguers*. In his quiet zeal to follow
logic to its inevitable conclusion, this sanguinary
bureaucrat falls just short of the excesses employed by
the "ethical madmen" Jack London describes in his
unfinished *The Assassination Bureau, Ltd.*, in which
logic doubles back on itself and becomes lunacy.

Although Helm and Mac can hardly be said to be
friends, their mutual respect is tremendous, and upon
at least two occasions (*The Intriguers, The Vanishers*),
Helm has seen fit to perform personal services for his
superior--provided they don't distract him from his
duty.

In the field, Matt Helm's enemies have included
Russian agents--among them the seductive Vadya, who
until her violent death was sometimes an ally, always a
killer, but in all capacities Helm's lover--Red Chinese
instruments, such as the rotund, Fu Manchu-ish Mr.
Soo, terrorists, South American dictators, domestic
revolutionaries, rival espionage outfits representing the
United States, and sometimes, as in *Murderers' Row*,
his own fellow agents. That field stretches from his
native New Mexico (*Death of a Citizen, The Silencers*,
others) to his ancestral Scandinavia (*The Wrecking
Crew, The Vanishers*, others), and all points between.
Loyalty and past associations count for nothing in his
homicidal sphere; no one is to be trusted, and nothing
is permanent. Longtime readers of the series, familiar
with the fates of friends and lovers, have become
resigned to the fact that it is no less lethal to be on
Helm's side than to oppose him.

Dyed-in-the-wool James Bond fans would be
disappointed by his weaponry, which includes standard
firearms, a pocket knife just a little larger than the
Boy Scout variety, a razor-edge belt buckle sheathed in
foil (for sawing one's way out of bondage), and a
dandy little packet with a hypodermic syringe and
three color-coded vials containing short-term and long-
term knockout agents and a deadly poison--referred to
early in the series as Agent Orange, anticipating the
dire properties later discovered in the defoliant by
that name used by Uncle Sam in Vietnam. Finally,
there is the trusty cyanide capsule intended for self-
immolation, concealed on each operative's body, never
mind where. At this writing, that device has been so

employed only once, by a fellow wrecking crew member
to release him from the agonies of a faceful of acid in
The Ravagers.

However, and despite his affection for edged
weapons, Helm places most of his faith in guns. He
prefers shotguns in close quarters (*The Terrorizers*),
sniper rifles with state-of-the-art telescopic sights for
long-range assassinations (*The Ambushers*), and a good
handgun in all other situations (any title). He eschews
Lugers for their Rube Goldberg firing mechanisms and
sneers at full automatic weapons, refusing to believe
that a stream of lead sprayed willy-nilly is superior to
one well-placed bullet. An ordinary maritime flare
pistol proves more than sufficient in *The Intriguers.*
In this area, Donald Hamilton once again draws upon
his own background. "Excuse me," says he, in *On
Guns and Hunting*, a non-Helm, nonfiction book about
his favorite avocations, "I love guns." He goes on:

> . . . hardly a hunting season passes that I
> don't hear a self-styled nature lover--generally
> an indignant female, at a cocktail party--express
> the hope that the cruel hunters invading the
> woods will shoot each other instead of the poor
> little deer. Somehow I'm not greatly impressed
> by the moral pretensions of a person who'll
> make a great issue of the right of animals to
> live while wishing for the death of human
> beings.

The sentiment echoes Hemingway writing in *Death in
the Afternoon* and appears in one form or another
throughout the Helm canon.

Matt Helm bears the Hamilton thumbprint. The
character has been germinating since long before the
series was conceived, and facets are visible in the
lonely heroes of Hamilton westerns, notably *Mad River*
and *The Big Country.* In the first, a man alienated

from his fellows by an unjust incarceration returns home and is forced to exchange his gentle nature for the violent tendencies of his murdered father and brother to set things right; in the second, a pilgrim come West to marry a ranch heiress must draw upon the rugged training of his seaman's past in order to prove himself among his new neighbors. Either of them, had he been born fifty years later, would have thought and behaved as Helm does. There is, in fact, a chronological bridge between the frontier gunman and the modern superspy in John Emmett, the young chemist who literally walks into danger in Hamilton's *noirish The Steel Mirror* (1948), and spends a hair-raising week fleeing a band of killers in the company of a beautiful young woman who may or may not be a homicidal maniac. Wondering whether or not the woman he's been spending time with will slide a knife between his ribs is a Matt Helm staple, and is at the core of *Assassins Have Starry Eyes*, predating the series as Hamilton's first foray into espionage fiction.

For all their plots, counterplots, body counts, and sinister females, the Helms are a good deal lighter than *noir*, mainly because of their hero's sardonic humor, on view almost constantly since the stories are told in first-person. These elements owe much to Raymond Chandler's forties-era private eye, Philip Marlowe. This stylistic debt was more in evidence in the early Helms, which began appearing only months after Chandler's death in 1959; but certain similar plot elements were still to be seen as late as 1971. Consider this scene from Chandler's *The Big Sleep* (1939):

> . . . He grunted something and the girl's body jerked hard, as though he had jammed a gun into her back. She came on again and drew near the lightless car. I could see him behind her now, his hat, a side of his face, the bulk of his shoulder. The girl stopped rigid and

screamed. A beautiful thin tearing scream that
rocked me like a left hook.

'I can see him!' she screamed. 'Through
the window. Behind the wheel, Lash!'

He fell for it like a bucket of lead. He
knocked her roughly to one side and jumped
forward, throwing his hand up. Three more
spurts of flame cut the darkness. More glass
scarred. . . .

I said: 'Finished?'

He whirled at me. Perhaps it would have
been nice to allow him another shot or two, just
like a gentleman of the old school. But his gun
was up and I couldn't wait any longer. Not long
enough to be a gentleman of the old school. I
shot him four times. . . .

Now compare it to this scene from Hamilton's
The Poisoners, published 32 years later:

He'd dragged Bobbie Prince out of the
Jeepster, and had pushed her down the road
ahead of him until they were clear of the
clouds of steam and other fumes billowing from
the crippled vehicle. Now he was standing there
with a gun--presumably his big .44 magnum
although I couldn't see it--thrust into her back.
. . .

'Drop it, Helm! Drop it or I'll shoot her!'

It was the same old tired routine. They
will keep on trying it. One day I'll have to sit
down and count how many times it's been tried
on me. . . .

I lifted my gun and shot him in the right eye.

The sole difference between the two scenes is Helm's refusal to rationalize. As it happens, the villain's gun discharges as he is falling, severely wounding his female hostage; a fact hardly worth noting, since her welfare is not important to Helm's mission. This attitude represents a purely duty-related conditioning that would have been anathema to Chandler's quixotic Marlowe. In all forms of crime fiction antedating *Death of a Citizen*, Matt Helm would have been a villain.

As previously indicated, the Helm books are not as dark and glowering as those of Graham Greene or John LeCarré, nor as depressingly prosaic as Len Deighton's. They move briskly in both the literal and the figurative sense; for Helm spends a great deal of time on the road. Most of the expository scenes take place while he is at the wheel, giving both Hamilton and his hero the opportunity to soliloquize at length upon the good and bad properties of various makes and models of automobiles, trucks, and vans, about which they have as much education and as many opinions as they have about guns. This is no random comparison, because vehicular mayhem is yet another Helm specialty. He is seldom more smug than when an antagonist forces him to drive to such-and-such a destination at gunpoint, musing upon the inadvisability of turning a deadly weapon upon someone and then placing him in charge of another just as deadly. Invariably the practice leads to grief for the practitioner. Similarly, Lord help the gun-wielding youngster conditioned by television to believe that a gun is a magic wand that will force anyone at whom it's directed to perform as desired. Guns are for killing.

The appearance of no style is the Hamilton style;

even the minimalism is minimal, presenting few handles
for the would-be pasticheur. There is a curious
sameness to the dialogue, a tendency toward eloquently
acerbic speeches on the part of world-weary assassin
and humanitarian ingenue alike. Dialogue tags are few.
Occasionally this is a fault, as when one homely "said"
would seem far less intrusive than the flock of "I
grimaceds," "she frowneds," and "he grinneds" that
Hamilton uses to break up lengthy monologues. In
addition, any reading of two or more Helm books in
succession reveals the author's fondness for the rather
obvious statement, "This is a lousy business." Yet
throughout the saga there is a refreshing lack of the
stylistic   narcissism   that   afflicts   the   European
intelligentsia, and none of the clumsiness that marks
the American globe-trotting school of Robert Ludlum
and William F. Buckley. Clearly Hamilton, like his
lanky, slightly lecherous alter-ego, is out to win no
contests save those concerned with endurance.

The typical Matt Helm plot calls for at least one
briefing in Mac's office; an attractive female traveling
companion,   preferably   non-violent--allowing   Helm
plenty of opportunity to debate the relative merits of
aggressive   and   passive   behavior--several   encounters
with dangerous types, some of them mere posturing
pussycats, the rest stone professionals like Helm; one
sanctimonious,   self-appointed   defender   of   decency,
hypocritical;   occasional   check-ins   with   Mac   by
telephone; a tryst with the traveling companion, who
has by this time proven her mettle despite her early
misgivings about violence; the capture, trussing, and
interrogation of Helm and friend by the villains, in the
course of which the prisoners learn far more than
their interrogators; an explosive and gory climax during
which all the villains are absented and accounted for,
with the possible exception of one admired opposite
number, with whom there will be a reckoning in some
later book; and, finally, a pairing-off with Helm and
either his companion or another delectable woman

whose acquaintance he has managed to make along the way, with the promise of more romantic but less dangerous adventures to follow. This formula, fairly rigid in comparison with most modern spy fiction, has not changed since the beginning, yet in Hamilton's hands delivers its share of surprises. (It is interesting to note that while the lone-wolf heroes of the American detective school as established by Dashiell Hammett and Raymond Chandler wind up each adventure alone, Matt Helm always has a date.)

Helm's age is difficult to assess. In 1960 he admitted to 36, but in the early 1970s he was "a gent in his forties." Since then he has ceased to count birthdays and seldom alludes to his World War II experience. Natural aging would make him 63 in 1987, the time of *The Demolishers*. However, heroes are not mortal and age on a sliding scale. He is always 6'4" and always weighs 200 pounds.

With the early exception of *Murderers' Row*, and beginning with the third book in the series (*The Removers*), Donald Hamilton switched to titles using nouns fashioned from intransitive verbs preceded by "the"--*The Shadowers, The Interlopers, The Detonators*, etc.--an unfortunate decision, making it difficult for even diehard aficionados to remember what title belongs to which plot. This practice almost certainly inspired the dreary succession of Exterminators, Pulverizers, and Liquidators whose numbered covers litter the paperback racks currently, wrapped around page after page of stuttering machine guns, slobbering entrails, and Neanderthal dialogue, written by armies of hacks under house names with their feet, and inevitably tarring the superior Hamiltons with a bloodstained brush. Also, with *The Revengers* (1982), the books bloated up from a lean 60,000 words to 100,000 and more, attaining bestseller heft at the sacrifice of word economy. This padding is most apparent in *The Annihilators*, which features mental telepathy, a South American witch doctor, and a mythical extinct civilization named after a famous brand of cheap dish sets. In a perfect world, a writer will write shorter books as he hones his skills; but as Matt Helm is fond of pointing out, our world is far from perfect. And even an overweight Eric is better than no Eric at all.

The Helm canon is at its electrifying best in the early numbers, including *Death of a Citizen*, *The Wrecking Crew*, *The Removers*, *The Silencers*, and *The Ambushers*; and there is a heartening return to the values (or, more correctly, conspicuous lack of them) that set the series apart from its predecessors and contemporaries in *The Detonators* (1985), *The Vanishers* (1986), and, most recently, *The Demolishers*. At all points in its progress, the collection is a homegrown cult classic, and despite the pesky omnipresence of the effete 007, the standard against which all paperback spy literature should be measured.

Checklist: Donald Hamilton

The Ambushers (Gold Medal, 1963)
The Annihilators (Gold Medal, 1983)
Assignment: Murder (Dell, 1956) (reprinted as
    Assassins Have Starry Eyes, Gold Medal, 1966)
The Big Country (Dell, 1957)
Death of a Citizen (Gold Medal, 1960)
The Demolishers (Gold Medal, 1987)
The Detonators (Gold Medal, 1985)
The Interlopers (Gold Medal, 1969)
The Intriguers (Gold Medal, 1973)
Mad River (Dell, 1956)
Murderers' Row (Gold Medal, 1962)
On Guns and Hunting (Gold Medal, 1970) (non-fiction)
The Poisoners (Gold Medal, 1971)
The Ravagers (Gold Medal, 1964)
The Removers (Gold Medal, 1961)

The Revengers (Gold Medal, 1982)
The Shadowers (Gold Medal, 1964)
The Silencers (Gold Medal, 1962)
The Steel Mirror (Rinehart, 1948) (hardcover)
The Terrorizers (Gold Medal, 1977)
The Vanishers (Gold Medal, 1986)
The Wrecking Crew (Gold Medal, 1960)

PETER RABE

by Donald E. Westlake

Peter Rabe wrote the best books with the worst titles of anybody I can think of. *Murder Me for Nickels. Kill the Boss Goodbye.* Why would anybody ever want to read a book called *Kill the Boss Goodbye*? And yet, *Kill the Boss Goodbye* is one of the most purely *interesting* crime novels ever written.

Here's the setup: Tom Fell runs the gambling in San Pietro, a California town of three hundred thousand people. He's been away on "vacation" for a while, and an assistant, Pander, is scheming to take over. The big bosses in Los Angeles have decided to let nature take its course; if Pander's good enough to beat Fell, the territory is his. Only Fell's trusted assistant, Cripp (for "cripple"), knows the truth, that Fell is in a sanitorium recovering from a nervous breakdown. Cripp warns Fell that he must come back or lose everything. The psychiatrist, Dr. Emilson, tells him he isn't ready to return to his normal life. Fell suffers from a manic neurosis, and if he allows himself to become overly emotional, he could snap into true psychosis. But Fell has no choice; he goes back to San Pietro to fight Pander.

This is a wonderful variant on a story as old as the Bible: Fell gains the world, and loses his mind. And Rabe follows through on his basic idea; the tension in the story just builds and builds, and we're not even surprised to find ourselves worried about, scared for, empathizing with, a gangster. The story of Fell's gradually deepening psychosis is beautifully done. The entire book is spare and clean and amazingly

unornamented. Here, for instance, is the moment when
Pander, having challenged Fell to a fistfight, first
senses the true extent of his danger:

> Pander leaned up on the balls of his feet,
> arms swinging free, face mean, but nothing
> followed. He stared at Fell and all he saw were
> his eyes, mild lashes and the lids without
> movement, and what happened to them. He
> suddenly saw the hardest, craziest eyes he had
> ever seen.

> Pander lost the moment and then Fell
> smiled. He said so long and walked out the door
> (page 47).

Kill the Boss Goodbye was published by Gold
Medal in August of 1956. It was the fifth Peter Rabe
novel they'd published, the first having come out in
May of 1955, just fifteen months before. That's a
heck of a pace, and Rabe didn't stop there. In the
five years between May 1955 and May 1960, he
published sixteen novels with Gold Medal and two
elsewhere.

Eighteen novels in five years would be a lot for
even a cookie-cutter hack doing essentially the same
story and characters over and over again, which was
never true of Rabe. He wrote in third person and in
first; he wrote emotionless hardboiled prose and
tongue-in-cheek comedy, gangster stories, exotic
adventure stories set in Europe and Mexico and North
Africa, psychological studies. No two consecutive
books used the same voice or setting. In fact, the
weakest Peter Rabe novels are the ones written in his
two different attempts to create a series character.

What sustains a writer at the beginning of his
career is the enjoyment of the work itself, the fun of
putting the words through hoops, inventing the worlds,

peopling them with fresh-minted characters. That enjoyment in the *doing* of the job is very evident in Rabe's best work.   But it can't sustain a career forever; the writing history of Peter Rabe is a not entirely happy one. He spent his active writing career working for a sausage factory. What he wrote was often pâté but it was packed as sausage--those titles!--and soon, I think, his own attitude toward his work lowered to match that of the people--agent, editors--most closely associated with the reception and publishing of the work. Rabe, whose first book had a quote on the cover from Erskine Caldwell ("I couldn't put this book down!"), whose fourth book had a quote on the cover from Mickey Spillane ("This guy is *good.*"), whose books were consistently and lavishly praised by Anthony Boucher in the *New York Times* ("harsh objectivity" and "powerful understatement" and "tight and nerve-straining"), was soon churning novels out in as little as ten days, writing carelessly and sloppily, mutilating his talent.

The result is, some of Rabe's books are quite bad, awkwardly plotted and with poorly developed characters. Others are like the curate's egg: parts of them are wonderful. But when he was on track, with his own distinctive style, his own cold clear eye unblinking, there wasn't another writer in the world of the paperback who could touch him. Of those first eighteen novels, a full seven are first-rate, another three are excellent at least in part, and eight are ordinary mushy paperbacks that could have been turned out by any junky hack with a typewriter.

The first novel, *Stop This Man*, showed only glimpses of what Rabe would become. It begins as a nice variant on the Typhoid Mary story; the disease carrier who leaves a trail of illness in his wake. The story is that Otto Schumacher learns of an ingot of gold loaned to an atomic research facility at a university in Detroit. He and his slatternly girl

friend Selma meet with his old friend Catell, just out
of prison, and arrange for Catell to steal the gold.
But they don't know that the gold is irradiated, and
will make people sick who are near it. The police
nearly catch Catell early on, but he escapes,
Schumacher dying. Catell goes to Los Angeles to find
Smith, the man who might buy the gold ingot.

Once Catell hides the ingot near Los Angeles, the
Typhoid Mary story stops, to be replaced by a variant
on *High Sierra*. Catell now becomes a burglar-for-hire,
employed by Smith, beginning with the robbery of a
loan office. There's a double-cross, the police arrive,
Catell escapes. The next job is absolutely *High Sierra*,
involving a gambling resort up in the mountains, but
just before the job Selma (Schumacher's girlfriend)
reappears and precipitates the finish. With the police
hot on his trail, Catell retrieves his gold and drives
aimlessly around the Imperial Valley, becoming
increasingly sick with radiation disease. Eventually he
dies in a ditch, hugging his gold.

The elements of *Stop This Man* just don't mesh.
There are odd little scenes of attempted humor that
don't really come off and are vaguely reminiscent of
Thorne Smith, possibly because one character is called
Smith and one Topper. A character called the Turtle
does tiresome malapropisms. Very pulp-level violence
and sex are stuck onto the story like lumps of clay
onto an already finished statue. Lily, the girl Catell
picks up along the way only to make some pulp sex
scenes possible, is no character at all, hasn't a shred
of believability. Selma, the harridan drunk who pesters
Catell, is on the other hand real and believable and
just about runs away with the book.

An inability to stay with the story he started to
tell plagued Rabe from time to time, and showed up
again in his second book, *Benny Muscles In*, which
begins as though it's going to be a rise-of-the-punk

history, a *Little Caesar*, but then becomes a much more
narrowly focused story. Benny Tapkow works for a
businesslike new-style mob boss named Pendleton.
When Pendleton demotes Benny back to chauffeur,
Benny switches allegiance to Big Al Alverato, an old-
style Capone type, for whom Benny plans to kidnap
Pendleton's college-age daughter, Pat. She knows
Benny as her father's chauffeur, and so will leave
school with him unsuspectingly. However, with one of
Rabe's odd bits of off-the-wall humor (this one works),
Pat brings along a thirtyish woman named Nancy
Driscoll, who works at the college and is a flirty
spinster. At the pre-arranged kidnap spot, Pat
unexpectedly gets out of the car with Benny, so it's
Nancy who's spirited away to Alverato's yacht, where
she seduces Alverato, and for much of the book Nancy
and Alverato are off cruising the Caribbean together.

The foreground story, however, remains Benny
and the problem he has with Pat. Benny doesn't know
Pat well, and doesn't know she's experimented with
heroin and just recently stopped taking it because she
was getting hooked. To keep Pat tractable, Benny
feeds her heroin in her drinks. The movement of the
story is that Benny gradually falls in love with Pat and
gradually (unknowingly) addicts her to heroin. The
characters of Benny and Pat are fully developed and
very touchingly real. The hopeless love story never
becomes mawkish, and the gradual drugged
deterioration of Pat is beautifully and tensely handled
(as Fell's deterioration will be in *Kill The Boss
Goodbye*). The leap forward from *Stop This Man* is
doubly astonishing when we consider they were
published four months apart.

One month later, *A Shroud for Jesso* was
published, in the second half of which Rabe finally
came fully into his own. The book begins in a New
York underworld similar to that in *Benny Muscles In*,
with similar characters and relationships and even a

similar symbolic job demotion for the title character,
but soon the mobster Jesso becomes involved with
international intrigue, is nearly murdered on a tramp
steamer on the North Atlantic, and eventually makes
his way to a strange household in Hannover, Germany,
the home of Johannes Kator, an arrogant bastard and
spy. In the house also are Kator's sister, Renette, and
her husband, a homosexual baron named Helmut.
Helmut provides the social cover, Kator provides the
money. Renette has no choice but to live with her
overpowering brother and her nominal husband.

Jesso changes all that. He and Renette run off
together, and the cold precise Rabe style reaches its
maturity:

They had a compartment, and when the
chauffeur was gone they locked the door, pushed
the suitcases out of the way, and sat down.
When the train was moving they looked out of
the window. At first the landscape looked flat,
industrial; even the small fields had a square
mechanical look. Later the fields rolled and
there were more trees. Renette sat close, with
her legs tucked under her. She had the rest of
her twisted around so that she leaned against
him. They smoked and didn't talk. There was
nothing to talk about. They looked almost
indifferent, but their indifference was the
certainty of knowing what they had (page 93).

The characters in *A Shroud for Jesso* are rich and
subtle, their relationships ambiguous, their story
endlessly fascinating. When Jesso has to return for a
while to New York, Renette prefigures the ending in
the manner of her refusal to go with him:

Over here Jesso, I know you, I want you, we
are what I know now. You and I. But over
there you must be somebody else. I've never

known you over there and your life is perhaps quite different. Perhaps not, Jesso, but I don't know. I want you now, here, and not later and somewhere else. You must not start to think of me as something you own, keep around wherever you happen to be. It would not be the same. What we have between us is just the opposite of that. It is the very thing you have given me, Jesso, and it is freedom (page 131).

And this opposition between love and freedom is what then goes on to give the novel its fine but bitter finish.

Rabe kept a European setting for his next book, *A House in Naples*, a story about two American Army deserters who've been black market operators in Italy in the ten years since the end of World War II. Charlie, the hero, is a drifter, romantic and adventurous. Joe Lenken, his partner, is a sullen but shrewd pig, and when police trouble looms, Joe's the one with solid papers and a clear identity, while Charlie's the one who has to flee to Rome to try (and fail) to find adequate forged papers. In a bar he meets a useless old expatriate American drunk who then wanders off, gets into a brawl, and is knifed to death. Charlie steals the dead man's ID for himself, puts the body into the Tiber under a bridge, then looks up and sees a girl looking down. How much did she see?

In essence, *A House in Naples* is a love story in which the love is poisoned at the very beginning by doubt. The girl, Martha, is simple and clear, but her clarity looks like ambiguity to Charlie. Since he can never be sure of her, he can never be sure of himself. Once he brings Martha back to Naples and the vicious Joe is added to the equation, the story can be nothing but a slow and hard unraveling. The writing is cold and limpid and alive with understated emotion, from

first sentence ("The warm palm of land cupped the
water to make a bay, and that's where Naples was"--
page 7) to last ("He went to the place where he had
seen her last"--page 144).

A House in Naples was followed by Kill the Boss
Goodbye, and that was the peak of Rabe's first period,
five books, each one better than the one before. In
those books, Rabe combined bits and pieces of his own
history and education with the necessary stock
elements of the form to make books in which tension
and obsession and an inevitable downward slide toward
disaster all combine with a style of increasing cold
objectivity not only to make the scenes seem brand
new but even to make the (rarely stated) emotions
glitter with an unfamiliar sheen.

Born in Germany in 1921, Rabe already spoke
English when he arrived in America at seventeen.
With a Ph.D. in psychology, he taught for a while at
Western Reserve University and did research at
Jackson Laboratory, where he wrote several papers on
frustration. (No surprise.) Becoming a writer, he
moved to various parts of America and lived a while in
Germany, Sicily and Spain. His first published work he
has described as "a funny pregnancy story (with
drawings) to McCall's." The second was Stop This
Man. In the next four books, he made the paperback
world his own.

But then he seemed not to know what to do with
it. Was it bad advice? Was it living too far away
from the publishers and the action? Was it simply the
speed at which he worked? For whatever reason,
Rabe's next six books were nearly as bad--except for
the middle of one of them--as the first five had been
good.

This began Rabe's first effort to develop a series
character, beginning with a book called Dig My Grave

Deep, which is merely a second-rate gloss of Hammett's *The Glass Key*, without Hammett's psychological accuracy and without Rabe's own precision and clarity. The book flounders and drifts and postures. The writing is tired and portentous, the characters thinner versions of Hammett's. The Ned Beaumont character is called Daniel Port, and at the end he leaves town in a final paragraph that demonstrates just how sloppy Rabe could get when he wasn't paying attention: "Port picked up his suitcases and went the other way. By the time it was full dawn he had exchanged his New York ticket for one that went the other way" (page 143).

That awkwardly repeated "other way" led directly into Rabe's next book, *The Out Is Death*, in which Port is now just a hero with a criminal background. The story is the one about the sick old ex-con forced to pull one last job by the sadistic young punk. Abe Dalton, the ex-con, is a well-realized character, a better version of Catell from *Stop This Man*, but Port, as Dalton's pal trying to help the old man out of trouble, is vague and uninteresting and never as tough as Rabe seems to think he is. Port, having started sub-Hammett, now becomes sub-W. R. Burnett.

After this second outing, Rabe left Port alone long enough to write *Agreement to Kill*, an odd book with a hokey beginning and not much finish at all but a fascinating long middle section. The book begins with Jake Spinner, a dirt farmer near St. Louis, coming out of jail after doing three years for assault. Rabe sets up Spinner as a victim in a land scheme being set up by the town's most important man, Dixon, but barely puts everything for that story in place when he suddenly switches gears. A professional hitman from the St. Louis mob kills Dixon. Spinner is blamed, but escapes and finds the killer stuck in his car, mired in a torn-up section of road. The killer convinces Spinner he'll never get justice in that town, so Spinner helps him get away and leaves with him. (The killer, with broken leg, can't drive.)

This killer is named Loma, and comes from Graham Greene's *This Gun for Hire*; Greene called him Raven. Loma is small, gray, clubfooted, quiet, ghostly, unemotional. A similar character, making a brief appearance in *Kill the Boss Goodbye*, was called Mound, and of course *loma* means "hill." The idea of Loma as a kind of mounded grave himself, silent and dead as a low hill, works well against the idea of Spinner endlessly spinning, flailing around, trying to save himself and always making things worse. Rabe's names are usually strange and frequently evocative, never more so than here.

The long middle section of *Agreement to Kill* is Rabe back in form at last, writing material that clearly interests him. Spinner, having decided he'll never make it in the straight world, has decided his only hope is to convince Loma to introduce him to the mob world, where maybe he'll be able to survive. Loma has no intention of introducing Spinner to anybody, but needs Spinner's help and thus strings him along.

Spinner, wanting to "change sides," to become an outlaw, tries to model himself on Loma's emotional emptiness. He has shoulder pains, that increase and become more and more crippling the more he suppresses his emotions. He meets a girl, Ann, the first true pulp non-entity female in Rabe's work since Lily in *Stop This Man*, and keeps pushing her away in his efforts to become emotionless.

Spinner does eventually meet a mob boss, and is given a job . . . to kill Loma. He welcomes this as a chance to show his progress toward coldness, and when Ann arrives just as he's planning to shoot Loma he feels he has to drive her away to demonstrate to himself his icy proficiency. At first, though she's hurt by what he says, she won't leave, and then:

> And then he knew she was crying even though there was no sound, and before it tore him open again--he thought about this very clearly--he lifted his hand and hit her in the face.
>
> A big star of pain exploded in his shoulder, making him tremble. It kept bursting, next to him, it kept shining all the time he could hear her feet running away and the way she breathed, running away down the road through the trees. He had reached such perfection in this that he walked to her car to make sure where she was (page 126).

"He had reached such perfection in this. . . ." I can't think of another writer who would have used that phrase. Nor who would have written this of Spinner's next thoughts, on his way to kill Loma:

> . . . Now for the business. It was a very small, surprisingly small matter to do this job now. That's the advantage of this new technique. Turn himself off and do a million things. Of course, one at a time, and each one --by comparison--very small, even unimportant. He walked to the cabin (page 126, 127).

But the pain in Spinner's shoulder keeps him from aiming his gun at Loma; finally he drops it on the floor, leaves, makes up with Ann, and they drive off together.

Loma turns Spinner in to the police for Dixon's murder. There's a trial, and Spinner's about to be convicted when Loma sends to the court his specially made boot for his club foot, which proves he was the murderer. This is all perfunctory, Rabe's interest clearly having been in the Spinner-Loma relationship. The man who spins all the time, alive but failing, and the man who is a silent cold hill, a mound, a filled-in grave.

After this semi-return to his powerful best, Rabe dropped right down again, with a third Daniel Port novel, *It's My Funeral.* Port seemed to be Rabe's (unconscious?) vehicle for derivative books imitating famous practitioners in the field. This time it's Leslie Charteris and the Saint, with Port involved in a tired story about the blackmailing of a movie star with the porno film she did years ago. Partway through, it switches to the equally tired story about the hotel with the hidden camera behind the two-way mirror. (That particular wheeze got another airing in the fine 1986 film *Mona Lisa*, showing that nothing is ever too old to be used again.)

Doing a fairly good imitation of Leslie Charteris' tongue-in-cheek comedy, Rabe has a subplot about a singer named Tess Dolphin that Port's trying to get into bed with; every time they near the sack, the story starts again, such as it is. The principal trouble here, apart from the slackness of the material, is that Port is not *involved.* Having no motivation for the central figure robs Rabe of his principal strength, which is the delineation of obsessed characters.

Rabe left Port again after this but remained in trouble for his next two books, both of which are flat and derivative and sloppily plotted. *Journey into Terror* combines the artificiality of plot of Cornell Woolrich at his worst with the overwrought emotions of James M. Cain at his worst, plus a dollop of David Goodis when the hero becomes a down-and-out drunk for a while. *Mission for Vengeance* keeps trying to be a John D. MacDonald novel, keeps almost making it, and keeps falling on its face. The villain, Farret, is rather like the villain in MacDonald's *Cape Fear*,

except that Farret keeps making threats and not
following through. *Mission for Vengeance* is also odd
for its use of first person narration. It was Rabe's
initial use of first person, and it appears only
sporadically, most of the book being in third person.
The jolts back and forth are irritating, and don't
accomplish much because the narrator-hero, John Miner
(indeed!), doesn't have much of a distinctive voice.

With his twelfth book, *Blood on the Desert*, Rabe
gets his second wind, goes for a complete change of
pace, and produces his first fully satisfying work since
Kill the Boss Goodbye. It's a foreign intrigue tale set
in the Tunisian desert, spy versus spy in a story filled
with psychological nuance. The characters are alive
and subtle, the story exciting, the setting very clearly
realized.

And, damn me, if it isn't followed by another
Daniel Port! In Rabe's own words, in a recent letter
to me, *Bring Me Another Corpse* is "a plot without
tension and some good writing thrown away in
disinterest." The best writing is at the very
beginning:

When the road flattened out toward Albany,
Daniel Port started to drive faster. For a short
while this distracted him, but there was an
unpleasant stiffness down his back, and his
hands were too tight on the wheel. At moments
the fast driving was like running away, though
Port didn't know what he was running from.

When the light was almost gone it started to
rain. The rain was thin and cold, but it put a
veil over the late-fall landscape.

Dan Port slowed a little and lit a cigarette.
The rain produced a feeling of shelter inside the
car. This feeling grew as it got darker, and

when he reached the outskirts of Albany Port felt easy enough to think of stopping and stretching his legs. He slowed for the next gas station and rolled up to the pumps. Then he got out.

The pumps sat in a big orb of light through which the rain showed like driving mist. The rain felt cold and wakeful and Port stood by the hood of the car while the station man let the gas hum into the tank. It was very quiet under the rain. The orb of light over the pumps illuminated a small area only, leaving the highway dark. A few cars passed there, each with two eyes of light and their tires writing signatures on the wet black asphalt.

The next car was just a murmur and a wet sound, because it went by so slowly. For a moment the gas station man thought the car meant to turn into the station, so he looked up. He saw his customer standing by the hood, smoking, hunching a little because of the rain-- and then he saw the cigarette spray up in the air. There was a sound like a whipcrack or a sharp rap with a stick on a wooden box, and the man spun suddenly, trying not to fall.

But Port began to bleed almost immediately. He dropped on the cement with a hard slam, which he didn't feel at all.

I quote so extensively the beginning of an otherwise undistinguished book because Peter Rabe is right; that *is* awfully good writing to be "thrown away in disinterest." A physical scene and an emotional ambience are sketched in with very deft strokes.

And what follows? At the end of Daniel Port's first novel, he'd protected himself from the mob bosses by leaving evidence to be given the police should he be killed. In *Bring Me Another Corpse*--what shriveled gnome thought *up* those titles?--someone who wants to make trouble for those bosses has realized the simplest way to do so is to kill Dan Port. Not a bad idea, but nothing *happens* in the book; just a lot of backing and filling.

Rabe followed this with *Time Enough to Die*, the last of the Daniel Port novels--whew!--and the only good one. The setting is the Mexican Pacific coast, mostly a small fishing village where a colony of immigrant Japanese fishermen live in their own separate neighborhood. There's a lot of local color, ocean and islands and jungle, all well done and well described. The plot is tricky without being artificial, and for once Rabe has surrounded Port with strong and interesting characters. *Time Enough to Die* is the last of the Port novels and the first of Rabe's final cluster of five excellent books.

The second of these, *My Lovely Executioner*, is another total change of pace, and a fine absorbing novel. Rabe's first book told completely in the first-person, it is also his first true *mystery*, a story in which the hero is being manipulated and has no idea why.

The hero-narrator, Jimmy Gallivan, is a glum fellow in jail, with three weeks to go on a seven-year term for attempted murder (wife's boyfriend, shot but didn't kill) when he's caught up in a massive jailbreak. He doesn't want to leave, but another con, a tough professional criminal named Rand, forces him to come along, and then he can't get back. Gallivan gradually realizes the whole jailbreak was meant to get *him* out, but he doesn't know why. Why him? Why couldn't they wait three weeks until he'd be released anyway? The mystery is a fine one, the explanation is believable and fair, the action along the way is credible and

exciting, and the Jim Thompsonesque gloom of the
narration is wonderfully maintained.

And next, published in May of 1960, Rabe's
sixteenth Gold Medal novel in exactly five years, was
Murder Me for Nickels, yet another change of pace,
absolutely unlike anything that he had done before.
Told in first person by Jack St. Louis, righthand man
of Walter Lippit, the local jukebox king, *Murder Me
for Nickels* is as sprightly and glib as *My Lovely
Executioner* was depressed and glum. It has a lovely
opening sentence, "Walter Lippit makes music all over
town" (page 5), and is chipper and funny all the way
through. At one point, for instance, St. Louis is drunk
when he suddenly has to defend himself in a fight: "I
whipped the bottle at him so he stunk from liquor. I
kicked out my foot and missed. I swung out with the
glass club and missed. I stepped out of the way and
missed. When you're drunk everything is sure and
nothing works" (page 164).

Nineteen-sixty was also when a penny-ante outfit
called Abelard-Schuman published in hardcover *Anatomy
of a Killer*, a novel Gold Medal had rejected, I can't
think why. It's third person, as cold and as clean as a
knife, and this time the ghostly unemotional killer,
Loma and Mound, is brought center stage and made
the focus of the story. This time he's called Jordan
(as in the river?) and Rabe stays in very tight on him.
The book begins,

When he was done in the room he stepped
away quickly because the other man was falling
his way. He moved fast and well and when he
was out in the corridor he pulled the door shut
behind him. Sam Jordan's speed had nothing to
do with haste but came from perfection.

The door went so far and then held back
with a slight give. It did not close. On the

floor, between the door and the frame, was the arm.

. . . he looked down at the arm, but then did nothing else. He stood with his hand on the door knob and did nothing.

He stood still and looked down at the fingernails and thought they were changing color. And the sleeve was too long at the wrist. He was not worried about the job being done, because it was done and he knew it. He felt the muscles around the mouth and then the rest of the face, stiff like bone. He did not want to touch the arm.

. . . After he had not looked at the arm for a while, he kicked at it and it flayed out of the way. He closed the door without slamming it and walked away. A few hours later he got on the night train for the nine-hour trip back to New York.

. . . But the tedium of the long ride did not come. He felt the thick odor of clothes and felt the dim light in the carriage like a film over everything, but the nine-hour dullness he wanted did not come. I've got to unwind, he thought. This is like the shakes. After all this time with all the habits always more sure and perfect, this.

He sat still, so that nothing showed, but the irritation was eating at him. Everything should get better, doing it time after time, and not worse. Then it struck him that he had never before had to touch a man when the job was done. Naturally. Here was a good reason. He now knew this in his head but nothing else changed. The hook wasn't out and the night-ride dullness did not come (pages 7-9).

It is from that small beginning, having to touch a victim for the first time, that Rabe methodically and tautly describes the slow unraveling of Jordan. It's a terrific book.

There was one other novel from this period, a Daniel Port which was rejected by Gold Medal and published as half of an Ace double-book in 1958, under the title *The Cut of the Whip.* Which brings to eighteen the books published between 1955 and 1960. Eighteen books, five years, and they add up to almost the complete story of Peter Rabe's career as a fine and innovative writer.

Almost. There was one more, in December of 1962, called *The Box* (the only Rabe novel published with a Rabe title). *The Box* may be Rabe's finest work, a novel of character and of place, and in it Rabe managed to use and integrate more of his skills and techniques than anywhere else. "This is a pink and gray town," it begins, "which sits very small on the North edge of Africa. The coast is bone white and the sirocco comes through any time it wants to blow through. The town is dry with heat and sand" (page 5).

A tramp steamer is at the pier. In the hold is a large wooden box, a corner of which was crushed in an accident. A bad smell is coming out. The bill of lading very oddly shows that the box was taken aboard in New York and is to be delivered to New York. Contents: "PERISHABLES. NOTE: IMPERATIVE, KEEP VENTILATED." The captain asks the English clerk of the company that owns the pier permission to unload and open the box. The box is swung out and onto the pier.

They stood a moment longer while the captain said again that he had to be out of here by this night, but mostly there was the silence by this night, but mostly there was the silence of heat everywhere on the pier. And whatever spoiled in the box there, spoiled a little bit more.

'Open it!' said the captain (page 11).

They open it, and look in.

'Shoes?' said the clerk after a moment. 'You see the shoes?' as if nothing on earth could be more puzzling.

'Why shoes on?' said the captain, sounding stupid.

What was spoiling there spoiled for one moment more, shrunk together in all that rottenness, and then must have hit bottom.

The box shook with the scramble inside, with the cramp muscled pain, with the white sun like steel hitting into the eyes there so they screwed up like sphincters, and then the man inside screamed himself out of his box (page 12).

The man is Quinn, a smartass New York mob lawyer who is being given a mob punishment: shipped around the world inside the box, with nothing in there but barely enough food and water to let him survive the trip. What happens to him in Okar, and what happens to Okar as a result of Quinn, live up to the promise of that beginning.

But for Rabe, it was effectively the end. It was another three years before he published another book, and then it was a flippant James Bond imitation called *Girl in a Big Brass Bed*, introducing Manny deWitt, an arch and cutesy narrator who does arch and cutesy dirty work for an international industrialist named

Hans Lobbe. Manny deWitt appeared twice more, in *The Spy Who Was 3 Feet Tall* (1966) and *Code Name Gadget* (1967), to no effect, all for Gold Medal. And Gold Medal published Rabe's last two books as well: *War of the Dons* (1972) and *Black Mafia* (1974).

Except for those who hit it big early, the only writers who tend to stay with writing over the long haul are those who can't find a viable alternative. Speaking personally, three times in my career the wolf has been so slaveringly at the door that I tried to find an alternative livelihood, but lacking college degrees, craft training or any kind of useful work history I was forced to go on writing instead, hoping the wolf would grow tired and slink away. The livelihood of writing is iffy at best, which is why so many writing careers simply stop when they hit a lean time. Peter Rabe had a doctorate in psychology; when things went to hell on the writing front, it was possible for him to take what he calls a bread-and-butter job teaching undergraduate psychology in the University of California.

It is never either entirely right or entirely wrong to identify a writer with his or her heroes. The people who carry our stories may be us, or our fears about ourselves, or our dreams about ourselves. The typical Peter Rabe hero is a smart outsider, working out his destiny in a hostile world. Unlike Elmore Leonard's scruffy heroes, for instance, who are always ironically aware that they're better than their milieu, Rabe's heroes are better than their milieu but are never entirely confident of that. They're as tough and grubby as their circumstances make necessary, but they are also capable from time to time of the grand gesture. Several of Peter Rabe's novels, despite the ill-fitting wino garb of their titles, are very grand gestures indeed.

Checklist: Peter Rabe

Agreement to Kill (Gold Medal, 1957)
Anatomy of a Killer (Abelard-Schuman, 1960)
    (hardcover)
Benny Muscles In (Gold Medal, 1955)
Black Mafia (Gold Medal, 1974)
Blood on the Desert (Gold Medal, 1958)
The Box (Gold Medal, 1962)
Bring Me Another Corpse (Gold Medal, 1959)
Code Name Gadget (Gold Medal, 1967)
The Cut of the Whip (Ace, 1958)
Dig My Grave Deep (Gold Medal, 1956)
Girl in a Big Brass Bed (Gold Medal, 1965)
A House in Naples (Gold Medal, 1956)
It's My Funeral (Gold Medal, 1957)
Journey into Terror (Gold Medal, 1957)
Kill the Boss Goodbye (Gold Medal, 1956)
Mission for Vengeance (Gold Medal, 1958)
Murder Me for Nickels (Gold Medal, 1960)
My Lovely Executioner (Gold Medal, 1960)
The Out Is Death (Gold Medal, 1957)
A Shroud for Jesso (Gold Medal, 1955)
The Spy Who Was 3 Feet Tall (Gold Medal, 1966)
Stop This Man (Gold Medal, 1955)
Time Enough to Die (Gold Medal, 1959)
War of the Dons (Gold Medal, 1972)

THE EXECUTIONER PHENOMENON

by Will Murray

In 1968, a former aerospace engineer with Naval combat experience in World War II and Korea named Donald Eugene Pendleton submitted a novel titled "Duty Killer" to a new publishing house. Early the next year, the novel was released as the first Pinnacle book, *The Executioner: War Against the Mafia*. It told the story of a Viet Nam era soldier who is called home to bury his parents and sister, only to discover their deaths are the result of having crossed the Pittsfield, Massachusetts branch of the Mafia. Mack Bolan vows to avenge their deaths and, applying the sniper skills he learned in Viet Nam, he begins a one-man war against organized crime that has subsequently carried him through over 100 books and several spin-off series.

The Executioner series became one of the true publishing phenomena of the 1970s paperback revolution. That it came as a result of an accident is of no importance. At that time, the paperback industry was moving from the drugstore racks into the burgeoning chain bookstore field. The dominant genres were war, westerns, romance, horror, science fiction and mystery. There was no adventure or action category as such. As a result, the predecessors to the Executioner pulp tradition were scattered in categories where they did not exactly belong. The Doc Savage series was shelved with science fiction books, and Award's Nick Carter usually ended up in the mystery racks, despite its more than casual parallels to Doc Savage.

The Executioner belonged in none of those

recognized categories. Although focusing on one
man's battle with crime, it was not a mystery or
detective series. Although it owed a great deal to
war fiction, it did not belong in the war category.
There was no science fiction to speak of in any of
the books. By default, the early Executioner titles
were categorized as mystery novels. It was not until
after the brisk sales of the early titles, and the
inevitable imitations sprang up, that action/adventure
emerged as a distinct category. Most of these early
rival series were put out by Pinnacle, which was a
former pornographic book house called Bee-Line Books
looking for legitimacy during the decline of print
pornography in the early 1970s. (Pendleton had been a
Bee-Line hack writing under another name before
creating Mack Bolan.) Pinnacle's first attempts to
duplicate the Executioner formula were Richard Sapir
and Warren Murphy's Destroyer, Joseph Rosenberger's
Death Merchant, Lionel Derrick's Penetrator, and
Stuart Jason's Butcher. Although there were
conceptual variations among each of these other
characters, most were launched as "war against crime"
series until other publishers, seeing the proliferation of
Pinnacle action series, flooded the market with their
own Executioner clones. By the mid-1970s, properties
like the Exterminator, the Eliminator, the Liquidator,
and the Sexecutioner were a glut on the market.
After that, the other Pinnacle series took on a kind of
protective coloration to differentiate themselves from
the pack. Only the Executioner and the Butcher
remained tied to their Mafia-busting roots.

It was after the explosion of such series that
the action/adventure category emerged as a separate
sub-genre, called by the trade "Male Action" books.
Its emergence led, ironically, to even more such
series, almost all of them numbered and issued at
regular intervals so that readers could anticipate each
release with the same confidence that they would
periodicals. If Don Pendleton was point man on this

strange new penetration of paperback book market, equal credit must be given to Pinnacle's Andrew Ettinger, the editor who conceived the Executioner format, which became so widely copied as to be an industry standard.

Despite the energizing effect caused by the Executioner series, it represents not an absolute beginning, but a coalescing of a pulp tradition that had existed before. Numbered paperback series were rare before the Executioner's debut, but not unknown. Bantam Books' Doc Savage, which consisted of reprints of the Street & Smith magazine hero popular in the 1930s, was the first consecutively numbered paperback series focusing on a single hero. It began late in 1964, but was anticipated by several months by what may be the first original paperback Male Action series, Award's Nick Carter.

Although the Nick Carter books were not numbered until the 1980s, the parallels between them and the Executioner are remarkable. The first Nick Carter title, *Run, Spy, Run*, was the first book to be released by Award Books--like Bee-Line/Pinnacle, a porn house looking for a legitimate publishing imprint. Where the Executioner was largely the vision of one man, Nick Carter was an updating of another Street & Smith pulp hero, packaged for Award by book producer Lyle Kenyon Engel, and written by an unbroken chain of writers. It's interesting that during the first years of the Executioner's high popularity, Nick Carter--an espionage/adventure series--flirted with several "Nick Carter against the Mafia" stories. As time has passed, the Executioner has grown more like Nick Carter than vice-versa. Ironically, the Executioners today are almost exclusively the work of a group of anonymous writers who ghost the series, some of them former Nick Carter writers.

But the actual roots of the Executioner have

nothing to do with packaging or format. Prior to writing the Executioner, Don Pendleton wrote a number of private eye novels under the pseudonym Stephan Gregory, many of which reveal a strong Mickey Spillane influence. Pendleton acknowledges the influence as seminal.

"If there has been any significant influence upon my work by other novelists then I would have to point to Mickey Spillane," Pendleton once told an interviewer. "There is a great deal more dimension to Spillane's stuff than most critics credit him with. He was the first to truly popularize the mean-bastard hero who still retained sentimental ideals about the worth of the human experience. Bolan is such a character. I was a very strong Spillane fan during his earlier years and I still believe him to be one of the most effective writers on the scene."

Many may disagree with Pendleton's assessment of Spillane, but there is no question that the Spillane influence on the Executioner and Don Pendleton is marked. Pendleton writes in a similarly white-heat violent style, substituting military jargon ("My recon is complete and target identification was positive") and macho bombast ("The hellfire trail had only just begun") for the private eye's traditional hard-boiled patter. Like Mack Bolan, Spillane's Mike Hammer is a war veteran who returns home to discover that the real enemy is not a foreign soldier, but home-grown crime. And as if to answer the title of Spillane's first Mike Hammer novel, *I, The Jury*, Mack Bolan is repeatedly quoted as boasting, "I am not their judge, I am their judgment. I am their Executioner." In this light, it seems clear that the Executioner and its rivals are all bastard children of the hard-boiled detective field by way of the adventure and war genres.

Despite these influences, Don Pendleton has found a voice and vision of his own and has remained true to it. Although his style might remind some of a truck driver who has read too much Mickey Spillane, it possesses a vitality and energy seldom found in more seasoned writers. His Mack Bolan is a single-minded man on a mission. There are seldom digressions from the action, even for sex. For a series written primarily for males and published by a former porn house, there is little sex, gratuitous or otherwise, in the Executioner books. Bolan has had a couple of girlfriends at different points in the series, but they seldom survive for very long. Ramboesque urban violence is the sum and substance of these books.

Mack Bolan lives for revenge. His extermination campaign against the Mafia--after the series' continuing characters and trappings were established in the first three novels--settled down into a one-man holy war against Mafia enclaves throughout America and Europe. The very titles reflect the progress of Bolan's crusade: *Detroit Deathwatch, Miami Massacre, Chicago Wipeout, California Hit* and many others.

The serial effect is no accident. As author Pendleton explained in a 1973 interview, "I took a sort of offbeat approach in the development of my series. It is done sort of like the old-time serials. There is definite continuity in each sequel. Actually the Executioner series is one long biographical novel chopped up into segments and turned out a piece at a time. As such, in my own mind, the full 15-book series as it stands today is actually an unfinished novel comprising, so far, 3,000 pages of print."

Critics have described Mack Bolan as a one-dimensional automaton, a mere killing machine driven by royalty payments and public fascination with the Mafia--thanks to the added impetus of Mario Puzo's 1969 novel, *The Godfather* (which first hit the racks only weeks ahead of the first Executioner), and its subsequent film adaptations. Pendleton seemed content to push the formula along for its first dozen books without tampering with it. Bolan was portrayed as a ruthless soldier operating outside the law in an urban war, whose impossible goal--the total extinction of the Mafia--was combined with a doomed, nihilistic philosophy. The hero who is hunted by all sides, who believes himself persecuted by the very people whose lives he is sworn to preserve, and who responds to a higher purpose and willingly surrenders all hope in the fulfillment of that purpose, is a very potent fantasy, especially to the young readers who represent a significant portion of the Executioner audience.

During the Depression, Popular Publications released over a hundred magazine novels featuring a similar hero, Richard Wentworth, who willingly lays aside all hope of marriage and normal life in order to eradicate crime as his alter-ego, the Spider, because he is compelled by some mystical higher calling to do so. Pendleton's Bolan may be an accidental rediscovery of that visionary hero approach.

A case could also be made that the Executioner books are a kind of pornography of violence in which the action scenes--brutal, violent and often gratuitously graphic--substitute for what in Pinnacle's Bee-Line titles would be the requisite sex scenes. Certainly the early Executioners are a series of bloody confrontations strung along a thin plotline. But no writer could churn out stories of endless unremitting violence without succumbing to boredom or criticism of his work, and it appears that after a dozen books, Pendleton felt the need to justify or legitimize his creation.

With the thirteenth novel, *Boston Blitz*, Pendleton first turns his attention to Bolan the man. Possibly the quintessential Executioner novel, *Boston Blitz* is a bloody excursion into Mack Bolan's *raison d'être*. It recounts his war of terror against the

Boston Mafia, who have kidnapped his surviving brother, Johnny, in an effort to draw Bolan out into the open. By this point in the series, Bolan has the Mafia so cowed that they are prepared to go to any lengths to extinguish his life.

Amid the carnage, a sharper vision of Mack Bolan begins to emerge, and it is subsequent to this novel that Pendleton starts mixing a larger than life, life-affirming philosophy into Bolan's dark nihilism. The philosophy is simplistic. The invoking of expressions like "Live Large!" and "Stay Hard!" are its paramount manifestations. It is also somewhat contradictory. Pendleton explained that Bolan had first earned his Executioner *nom de guerre* as a combat sniper in Viet Nam, then adds in later books that he was also known as "Sergeant Mercy" because of his work tending injured Vietnamese peasants. Pendleton sometimes gives the appearance of wanting to have it both ways with his mean-bastard hero.

As the series progressed, the preoccupation with the inner workings of the Mafia--which was a big part of the series--was de-emphasized in favor of an expansion of the series' military aspects. Bolan's private arsenal expanded from hand pistols and sniper rifles to anti-tank weapons, shoulder-fired rockets and an increasing array of high-tech military equipment. Perhaps in answer to the Dirty Harry films, Bolan took as his personal sidearm the most powerful handgun ever made, the .44 Automatic Magnum, his signature AutoMag.

If anything, the books sold better than before. But in the midst of this success, Pendleton and Pinnacle had a falling out. When the sixteenth Executioner was published in 1973, it bore the title *Sicilian Slaughter* and a new byline, Jim Peterson. Pendleton had decided to take his character to a larger publisher, Signet. Pinnacle, because they could not come to terms with Pendleton, decided to continue the series without the author, on the theory that because it was their editorial staff who created the format of the series, they actually owned the rights to the name Executioner. "Jim Peterson" was really William Crawford, and *Sicilian Slaughter* was recognized by Executioner readers as inferior to Pendleton's vision of Mack Bolan. Pinnacle ended up settling in Pendleton's favor and, in 1975, the series resumed with Pendleton writing.

Stylistically, the Bolan books became leaner and given to a lot of one-sentence paragraphs, internal monologue and endless repetitions of semi-literate sentences (and sentence fragments) like: "One of those guys was, yeah, Crazy Marco," and "Yeah, even overloaded bladders wanted to let go at dawn," and "Necessary, though, yeah."

It was inevitable, given the formula of moving Mack Bolan from city to city, effectively annihilating the underworld infra-structure wherever he went, that Pendleton would run out of locales and plots--if public interest in Mafia-busting and/or Mack Bolan did not wane first.

Eventually, the war against the Mafia formula did wear thin, and beginning with book number thirty-three, *Monday's Mob*, Pendleton initiated a six-book sequence in which Bolan is offered a pardon for his "crimes" and a position as the head of a White House-run counter-terrorist unit. Bolan accepts the post because by this time he has *La Cosa Nostra* on its knees. But he asks for a six-day grace period in which to finish off the Mob. Bolan's long-anticipated "last mile" began in *Monday's Mob*, continued in *Terrible Tuesday* and four other similarly-titled books. When it wrapped up, a year and a half later in *Satan's Sabbath*, Pendleton would have us believe that Mack Bolan had extinguished the

Mafia in six days, and Bolan stood on the threshold of a new life and a new mandate: to fight terrorism the world over. It was just before this final Pinnacle period that Don Pendleton first began using ghost writers to help him turn out his books--a probable indication of waning interest in his own character--but he wrote the entire last mile sequence himself.

As the series was poised on the brink of a major new direction, the old ownership conflict between Pinnacle and Don Pendleton resurfaced. Pendleton decided to take the series to a new publisher, Gold Eagle, an arm of Harlequin Books, but a lawsuit prevented implementation of that plan for over a year while the question was fought in the courts.

After it was resolved in Pendleton's favor, Mack Bolan returned as a Gold Eagle series. For legal purposes, the series was renamed Mack Bolan, but paradoxically, Bolan operated under a new name, John Phoenix, which was meant to symbolize his new life. The old Pinnacle numbering was continued. Pendleton did not continue, however. His role was limited to overseeing the property. And a property it became. Mack Bolan has since seesawed through different working situations, at first operating as an officially-sanctioned counter-terrorist but later reverting to his old outlaw status and even taking the occasional foray against the re-emerging Mafia.

Bolan referred to it as his "New War," but the fires of the old war had been replaced by a less personal campaign against what the reading public perceived as a graver menace than mere street criminals. The books, which had been released on a quarterly basis at Pinnacle, quickly jumped to monthly frequency, sacrificing the multiple editions of the old Pinnacle backlist (now out of print) for more novels selling fewer copies. But Mack Bolan continued to sell briskly. Characters introduced in early books have

been spun off into two ghost-written series of their
own, Phoenix Force and Able Team, in which Bolan
puts in the rare token appearance. The military
orientation has completely swamped all three series,
and eventually Don Pendleton's name was taken off the
Bolan books, signifying perhaps that Pendleton does
not see them as entirely authentic.

Even in this format, Pendleton's series has
remained the trail-blazer. Aided by the bankruptcy of
Pinnacle Books in 1984, most of the original
Executioner imitators have either ceased or gone to
other publishers, no trace of their Pinnacle origins
remaining. Spearheaded by the Able Team and
Phoenix Force spin-offs, the male action category has
been virtually given over to Viet Nam War or
counter-terrorist series. The change has been so
profound that a decade after Mack Bolan declared a
final victory in his war against the Mafia, no series
exists today which relies on that format. And firmly
fixed in the new order, a fresh Mack Bolan novel
continues to be issued every month.

Checklist: Don Pendleton

Boston Blitz (Pinnacle, 1972)
California Hit (Pinnacle, 1972)
Chicago Wipeout (Pinnacle, 1971)
Detroit Deathwatch (Pinnacle, 1974)
Miami Massacre (Pinnacle, 1970)
Monday's Mob (Pinnacle, 1978)
Satan's Sabbath (Pinnacle, 1980)
Terrible Tuesday (Pinnacle, 1979)
War Against the Mafia (Pinnacle, 1969)

WARREN MURPHY AND HIS HEROIC ODDBALLS

by Dick Lochte

There's a difference between those earlier pulp writers and Dick [Sapir] and myself. It deals directly with the differences between the novels of plot and the novels of character. The old pulps were stories of plot. The characters were fixed, immutable. Our characters, Remo and Chiun, are always changing. Remo has gone from being a super-patriot to someone who's totally disillusioned because he knows the system doesn't work. Chiun longs to retire to a place where they grow melons and know how to treat assassins, but in the new book, he begins to feel that this government is appreciating his talents more. I'm not sure if the two of them are growing, but they're moving all the time. That makes it difficult for the writer, because you have to go beyond technique. You start pulling moods and feelings out of yourself to put into your characters. You can make them funny, but the process itself gets pretty serious.

--Warren Murphy, in an interview with the author, January, 1978.

The final page of the paperback novel, *Trace* (Signet, October 1983), identifies its writer as follows: "Warren Murphy is the author of more than sixty novels and screenplays, including the satiric adventure series *The Destroyer*, with more than 25 million copies in print. He is a former newspaperman and political-campaign consultant whose hobbies are chess, mathematics, and martial arts. He lives in Teaneck, New Jersey."

Since that time, Murphy has married, fathered a son, moved to a new home, also in New Jersey, and pushed his output of novels and screenplays past the ninety mark. This prodigious fiction total is even more remarkable when one considers that Murphy didn't sell his first book until 1971.

It was considerably earlier than that, in 1963 to be precise, that Murphy, a secretary to the Mayor of Jersey City, New Jersey, and Richard Sapir, a reporter he'd met hanging around Jersey City Hall, decided to collaborate on a novel in the Ian Fleming mode. Writing alternate chapters, they quickly completed a yarn about a policeman from their state who is framed for murder, executed and mysteriously revived to become the perfect assassin, a man who no longer exists, for CURE, a secret U.S. organization approved by then-President John F. Kennedy.

They then sat back and waited for it to be sold and published. They waited eight years.

During that time, book editors and literary agents came and went, Sapir left the newspaper business and Murphy watched his associates in government get involved in a political scandal that sent most of them to jail. And, not incidentally, a paperback publishing house named Pinnacle had begun mining a relatively new reader market with Don Pendleton's unstintingly violent tales of a man at war with the Mafia, *The Executioner* series.

In 1971, Sapir's father, a dentist, talked proudly of his son's manuscript to a patient who agreed to show it to the editors at the publishing house where she worked, Pinnacle. Before the year was out, *The Destroyer* series was launched, along with the fiction-

writing careers of Murphy and Sapir. Their
collaboration on the series, an odd one at best, as we
shall see, continued on and off until Sapir's death in
1987.

After thirty-six volumes of *The Destroyer*, Sapir
decided to devote his time to hardcover novels, while
Murphy, in his words, "made the value judgment that
I could make a lot more money by continuing to write
paperbacks. This was at a time when hardcover books
weren't selling. I was young and I was ready to write
a lot of books and take the money and not think twice
about it." (1)

He penned many *Destroyer* titles himself,
oversaw and reworked others and, in between, created
three more softcover series--the adventures of two
hard-charging, screwball cops, Razoni and Jackson
(Pinnacle), who-done-its involving Digger, a free-
wheeling Las Vegas insurance investigator who divides
his time among placating his Chinese-Italian girlfriend,
arguing with his boss, padding his expense accounts,
getting blotto and solving murders (for Pocket) and
Trace (for NAL), a reworking of Digger with the names
changed to protect the copyright.

Leonardo's Law, a locked-room mystery, was
penned as a probable series. But its publishing house
neglected to ship the book from the warehouse, which,
Murphy notes, "practically guarantees that the book
will not sell many copies." (2) Its series potential will
be better evaluated following the 1988 reissue of the
novel by the Canadian publisher, PaperJacks.

Additionally, Murphy has delivered a quartet of
mainstream novels: *Atlantic City* for Pinnacle (an
original work with no connection to the film of the
same title that appeared later); *The Red Moon*, and
The Ceiling of Hell, for Fawcett; and, in collaboration
with his wife, Molly Cochran, who had assisted in an

even dozen of the later Destroyer tales, he created
Grandmaster for Pinnacle, an ambitious and complex
tale of espionage and mysticism.

Early in 1987, Murphy decided to join the ranks
of the Donalds, John D. Mac-, Gregory Mc-, and - E.
Westlake, and the others who have put their
paperback original days behind them. Due to the
bankruptcy of his first publisher, Pinnacle, he had
just spent nearly two years embroiled in litigation
over the rights to the first fifty-eight Destroyer
novels, as well as to contracts for future books.
Present plans called for Zebra Books to eventually
reprint those editions and to assume a contract
calling for three hardcover spy novels. Additionally,
he and Molly Cochran had signed hardcover-softcover
deals with NAL for three other novels, including the
remaining two parts of a Grandmaster trilogy.

He still would be represented in softcover,
however. Before Sapir died, he and Murphy signed a
new contract with NAL that is allowing *The Destroyer*
series to continue beyond Remo and Chiun's seventieth
outing. Those books carry the credit "created by
Warren Murphy and Richard Sapir" and are being
ghost-written by others, primarily novelist Will Murray
(3) who ghosted earlier adventures and compiled and
edited *The Assassin's Handbook* (Pinnacle, November
1982), an assortment of odds and ends related to the
series (including an informative interview with the
authors and the only known novella dealing with the
characters, a retelling of the origin of the series,
titled *The Day Remo Died*).

In 1985, *Remo, The Adventure Begins* . . . was
released by Orion Pictures. The movie was designed
to provide Remo and Chiun with the same sort of
international fame that *Dr. No* brought to James Bond.
But while Joel Grey proved to be an impressive
approximation of the wily and argumentative Chiun,

and Fred Ward made a passable lunkheaded Remo, the
plot was weaker by far than any of the sixty or so
Murphy and Sapir books that the filmmakers might
have adapted. (In any case, Pinnacle had closed down
by that time, and had a hoard of happy moviegoers
been turned loose suddenly on the bookstands, they
would have discovered that the first fifty-eight books
in the series were no longer available.)

At present, a pilot, again starring Grey, is being
prepared for ABC-TV. But, even without that sales
impetus, as the cover of #69, *Blood Ties* (Signet,
August 1987), declared, there were "over 20 million
copies [of The Destroyer novels] in print." That
number should increase dramatically when Zebra
eventually reissues the first fifty-eight titles.

*

We've got an eight-book contract that calls
for a Destroyer every three months for the next
two years. Since Dick takes about a month for
his ninety-five pages, and I take a month for
mine, that works fine for us.

--Warren Murphy, in an interview
with the author, January, 1978.

Any series that can sail through seventy novels in
only sixteen years, surviving the bankruptcy of its
original publisher and the untimely passing of one of
its creators, must have something going for it.
Especially when you consider that its debut book was
not meant to be a series at all.

Neither *Created, The Destroyer*, nor its sequel,
Death Check, bears much resemblance to the rest of
the adventures of Remo and his adopted father,
Chiun, the Master of the House of Sinanju. It is the
byplay between these two characters, combined with

often savage satire on contemporary life and lifestyles,
that sets Remo and Chiun apart from the other
paperback vigilantes who proliferated in the early
Seventies but ran out of firepower before the decade
had ended. Murphy and Sapir provided their super
heroes with a secret weapon--humor.

In *Created*, Chiun is a karate instructor, a minor
player of considerably less importance to the plot
than the lemony Dr. Harold Smith, CEO of CURE, the
secret organization that conscripts Remo into its
employ. And the tone of the novel is surprisingly
straightforward and even a bit pretentious. The
opening line, for example, "Everyone knew why Remo
Williams was going to die," was Sapir's bow to Stephen
Crane's line, "No one knew the color of the sky." (4)
The title itself, a quote from the *Bhagavad Gita* (5),
was to be taken literarily, not literally. Neither
Murphy nor Sapir intended for "The Destroyer" to
become Remo's working title. "That was Pinnacle's
idea," Murphy says. "We would probably have sold
more copies if it had been 'The Remo series,' and had
not been lumped in with the other guys." (Those other
guys, The Executioner, The Butcher, The Cameleon,
Pinnacle heroes all, are splendidly spoofed in *Bay City
Blast*, #38 [Pinnacle, October 1979], in which Remo and
Chiun, attempting to halt a Syndicate takeover of an
American city, are thwarted by four amateurs at war
with the mafia: the wealthy Samuel Arlington Gregory,
aka The Eraser, and his Rubout Squad consisting of a
grumpy Viet vet nicknamed The Exterminator, a fellow
with vague underworld connections called The Baker,
and a boozy actor, The Lizard.)

When Pinnacle reprinted *Created, The Destroyer*
in 1976, it included a new foreword by Chiun that
offers evidence of the mood swing that the series
went through after its straightforward start. The
Master of Sinanju notes: "I appear briefly in this
shoddy manuscript. The scribblers, Sapir and Murphy,

describe me as a karate teacher. To call the art of
Sinanju karate is to call the noontime sun a flashlight.
So much for Sapir and Murphy." Chiun ends with the
advice, "THROW THIS BOOK AWAY. It will do you no
good."

The same might be said for #2, *Death Check*
(Pinnacle, January 1972), in which Sapir and Murphy
still had not quite hit upon the proper formula. But
in *Chinese Puzzle* (Pinnacle, March 1972), #3 in the
series, the magic happened. Its plot, about a U.S.
President's visit to China, is spiced with hilarious
satire. (Oddly enough, it arrived at the newsstands
the same week that Richard Nixon really did go to
China.) And the authors began to explore the father-
son relationship of Chiun to Remo, providing readers
with information about the ancient's past and the
history of the glorious House of Sinanju, birthplace of
the world's most revered assassins.

The editors at Pinnacle weren't overjoyed by the
new direction the books were taking. According to
Murphy: "They told us to put in more blood and guts
and less humor. Dick and I went out and got
swacked and said, screw it, we were going to write
the books the way we wanted to." (6)

By #3, they had begun their unusual method of
collaboration. Sapir would write the outline and the
first half of the manuscript and turn them over to
Murphy, who would complete the story and give it a
final polish. But, Murphy recalls, the working
relationship was a rocky one and, after Sapir wrote
#7, *Union Bust* (Pinnacle, January 1973), single-
handedly, and Murphy soloed on #8, *Summit Chase*
(Pinnacle, February 1973), they "had some kind of a
flap, and . . . communicated through a joint business
agent. One of the books--I think it was #9, *Murder's
Shield* (Pinnacle, April 1973), was written with no
communication at all. Dick did his ninety-five pages,

and he stopped at the bottom of page ninety-five in the middle of a sentence, in the middle of a freaking word. Sent me the ninety-five pages without an outline, without anything." (7)

Still, even this bizarre system worked in mysterious ways. In *Terror Squad*, #10 (Pinnacle, June 1973), Sapir concocted a Sinanju legend involving a "place of the dead animals." It was up to Murphy to figure out that this "place," a setting for the confrontation between Remo and one of the series' better continuing villains, Chiun's traitorous first pupil, Nuihc, had to be The Museum of Natural History in New York.

#11, *Kill or Cure* (Pinnacle, August 1973), a strong addition to the series, brings Remo and Chiun to Miami, where the old Korean immediately falls in with a group of Jewish mothers, proudly telling them tales of *his* son, while Remo pursues a threat to a statewide election. Murphy notes: "Dick was writing about his parents and I was writing about politics and everything mingled very well." (8)

#18, *Funny Money* (Pinnacle February 1975), introduces another terrific villain, the apparently unstoppable Mr. Gordons, whose method of violence is so confusing to Chiun that he becomes worried for Remo's safety. He unsuccessfully tries to get his "son" to turn his back on Gordons and his threat to the American monetary system, and return with him to Sinanju. He fails, and together they discover the secret of what makes Gordons tick. But in *Assassins Play-Off*, #20 (Pinnacle, September 1975), probably the best of all of *The Destroyers*, Remo accompanies Chiun to the Korean village of Sinanju for a final confrontation with Nuihc.

Once the books enter the double digits, each volume sees Remo changing, his physical prowess

improving under Chiun's tutelage and his mental
attitudes altering. He is fulfilling the legend that has
kept the old man at his side, the legend of the white
man who will eventually assume his rightful place as
the master of Sinanju. In #20, both men realize the
strong bond that has grown between them. And it
becomes very apparent that, no matter how frantic or
far-fetched their plots, Sapir and Murphy had taken
special care to make the relationship and the feelings
that flow between Remo and Chiun totally believable.

By then, *The Destroyer* books were appearing at
a rate of one every three months and other writers
were brought in to help make the deadlines. "Some
of it was second-rate help," Murphy admitted. "Books
25, 27 and 29, *Sweet Dreams* (Pinnacle, October 1976),
The Last Temple (Pinnacle, March 1977) and *The Final
Death* (Pinnacle, July 1977--about Chinese vampires,
for God's sake--were the worst books we've ever
done." (9)   But in #30, *Mugger Blood* (Pinnacle, July
1977), the series bounded back with a surprisingly
hard look at America's apathy over street crime.

Murphy has acknowledged the contribution that
their editor at Pinnacle, Andrew Ettinger, made to the
success of the series. "He kept us on track, told us
when to cut back or move ahead, though Dick always
hated him. At the very least, he read the books.
When he was replaced, and there was a change at the
company, the new people didn't bother. They knew
what the books were about because they looked at the
covers. That's when we got into writing forewords
that told readers not to buy the books, not to
encourage the lunatics at Pinnacle to continue. No
one there read the books. They didn't know. And the
less they read, the nastier we got." (10)

In 1979, Sapir decided to concentrate on other
projects and Murphy took over the series with #37,
Bottom Line (Pinnacle, July 1979), without any

noticeable change in plotting or characterization.
Ghost writers, including Will Murray, Robert Randisi
and Molly Cochran, began working on the series, but,
probably because Murphy provided an outline and the
final polish, all of the books remained of a piece.

Actually, Sapir never quite abandoned *The
Destroyer*. He returned to co-author #48, *Profit
Motive* (Pinnacle, April 1982), about a bacterium that
eats the world's oil supply; #52, *Fool's Gold* (Pinnacle,
May 1983), in which nations struggle to learn the
location of a mountain of gold; and #55, *Master's
Challenge* (Pinnacle, February 1984), in which assassins
from three tribes try to destroy Remo. In each case,
Pinnacle marked the reteaming by labeling the books
"supernovels" and raising their cover price.

In December of 1984, Pinnacle published its last
new Destroyer novel, #58, *Total Recall*, a Murphy solo
effort, but a month previously, New American Library
had already brought out #59, *The Arms of Kali*. Co-
authored by Murphy and Sapir, it is an entertaining
entry involving an ancient goddess who is using
fanatical teenage followers to befriend and murder
airplane passengers.

The Murphy and Sapir collaborations for Signet
have been among the best in the series. *Remo, The
Adventure Begins ...* (Signet, October 1985), credited to
both authors but actually written by Sapir, is an
adaptation of Christopher Wood's depressingly
mundane script for the motion picture. Sapir's breezy
style is as readable as always, but he was obviously
hindered by a storyline not of his making.

At one point, the authors decided to end the
Destroyer saga with its seventieth entry. Murphy
says: "I wrote a book called *Their Final Bow*. I had
Remo and Chiun go back to Sinanju, with Chiun dying
and Remo quitting CURE. NAL wanted to use ghosts,

instead. So we changed the title to *The Eleventh Hour* and made a couple of little changes at the end so that the ghost-writer, Will Murray, could be able to pick it right up and with a little bit of a segue--Remo goes back to work and Chiun's death is revealed as a scam to get Remo to marry a hideous woman from the village--the series would continue." (11)

*

Basically, I've always made a living writing about heroes who were a little bit dopey.

--Warren Murphy, in an interview with the author, May, 1987.

In February of 1982, Pocket Books debuted Murphy's *Digger* series with not one but two full-length books, *Smoked Out* and *Fools Flight*. A third Digger, *Dead Letter*, arrived in April and the fourth and last, *Lucifer's Weekend*, in October. The covers of these books indicate that neither the artist nor the copywriter had bothered to read them. Their hero, Julian Burroughs, aka "Digger" because of his persistence in digging up evidence of insurance frauds, is depicted as a very handsome, very thoughtful young fellow with dark hair. Beneath his logo is a composite of various action sequences--fistfights, shootings, planes exploding--and romantic trysts. A fixed caption reads: "A new action adventure series from the author of *The Destroyer*."

Murphy describes Digger as being six-foot-three, thirty-eight, blond and, usually, drunk. Digger never looks thoughtful, because he isn't. He's witty and loves double-entendres and can quip with the best of them. But he actually blunders through his insurance investigations, annoying men and wooing women, while secretly recording their conversations on cassettes via a little gold frog tie tack. Digger eventually listens to the tapes, but he can never make any sense of them. However, his Oriental-Italian girlfriend, Koko, who monitors the cassettes primarily to keep tabs on Digger's rather woozy, boozy behavior, invariably discovers from them the clues necessary to solve the crimes.

This is not an action-adventure series, any more than are the works of Doyle, Stout or Chandler. Very few action sequences are described. Mainly these are mysteries, who-done-its that play fair with the reader. What separates them from the more conventional novels of detection are their hilarious situations and dialogue, and their characters, on which Murphy spends more time than most mystery writers.

For example, in all of Rex Stout's novels about Nero Wolfe and Archie Goodwin, one has difficulty recalling any mention of Archie's family. In Digger's debut case, we discover that he likes his father, a retired policeman, but has trouble being in the same room with his mother. He is divorced and tries to stay on the West Coast rather than run the risk of bumping into his ex-wife or his children, whose names he can't remember.

His relationship with Koko is just as unique. Forget Nick and Nora Charles or Pam and Jerry North, or even *Moonlighting*'s Maddie Hayes and David Addison. Digger and Koko live together in his high-rise apartment in Las Vegas, but she refuses to give up a casino job that consists mainly in dealing cards, but also includes a little hooking on the side. Somehow Murphy makes it all not only palatable but, in an odd way, poignant. He has been equally successful in discovering a new way to mix murder with mirth without stooping to spoof the genre.

In October of 1983, precisely a year after Pocket Books published the final Digger, NAL released

Murphy's new series, *Trace*. This was, actually, a
continuation of the Diggers but, as Murphy explained,
"NAL didn't want to pick up somebody else's used
series." (12) So insurance investigator Julian
Burroughs, Digger, became insurance investigator Devlin
Tracy, Trace, complete with lovable father and
peevish mom, feared ex-wife and vaguely-recalled
children. As was the case with Digger, his immediate
supervisor at the insurance company loathes him but
has to tolerate him because the president of the
company finds Trace amusing.

Trace lives with the Japanese-Sicilian Chico, and
in the early novels their situation remains the same as
Digger's and Koko's. But as the detective staggers
through his next several capers, *Trace and 47 Miles of
Rope* (Signet, April 1984), *When Elephants Forget*
(Signet, October 1984), and *Once a Mutt* (Signet,
April 1985), the characters start to change. Trace, at
Chico's behest, cuts back on his drinking and both
behave more monogamously. He even becomes more
tolerant of his mother.

Meanwhile, there is no stinting on the mystery
or humor elements. And, there are enough of
Murphy's off-the-wall satiric touches to make each
book worth reading. On page 24 of *Elephants*, for
example, while attempting to solve a case involving a
syndicate hood and his son and while trying to help
his own father through an emotional crisis, Trace
decides to use Robert Parker's gourmet hero, Spenser,
as his guide to becoming a successful sleuth. He
explains to a man sitting next to him on a plane:

'I'm a private detective. We're all great
cooks.'

'I didn't know that,' the man said.

'You probably don't read enough,' Trace said.

'Right from Nero Wolfe on. We're all good cooks. Hell, even Sherlock Holmes. Except he mostly cooked up cocaine.'

'I read Mike Hammer. I don't think Mike Hammer ever cooked,' the man said warily.

'Well, that was Mike Hammer. What did he know? I tell you. If he'd cooked, he'd still be going strong. Instead of being reduced to beer commercials.'

In *Pigs Get Fat* (Signet, October 1985), his fifth investigation, Trace takes Chico to San Francisco to solve the disappearance of a wealthy insured who lived for sex. In addition to the complexities and peculiarities of the case, he is forced to participate in a convention of Japanese-Americans with Chico's mother, Mrs. Mangini.

There, he confides to Chico, he feels

'about as welcome as a survivor from the Bataan Death March.'

'Bataan,' the man next to him said aloud. His face broke into a big smile. 'You in Bataan, too?'

'Yes,' Trace lied.

'I too. I not see you.'

'I spent most of my time hiding in ditch.'

'Sorry I missed you,' Mr. Nishimoto said. (13)

Near the end of the novel, Mr. Nishimoto, who turns out to be the convention's guest of honor, the wealthiest Japanese-American in the country, addresses the huge assembly and reads a poem he has composed. Chico informs Trace:

'The poem is about his friend, a great warrior who crushed the enemy under his feet, like beetles, during that great battle.'

There was rousing applause. Mr. Nishimoto bowed politely, then continued speaking.

'He says his friend is with us now,' Chico translated for Trace. 'And the name of this hero of Japan is . . .'

Mr. Nishimoto shouted, 'Dev-u-rin Tracy.'

Everyone in the room jumped to their feet and bowed in Trace's direction.

Mrs. Mangini's eyes filled with tears. 'I never know you fight on our side in war,' she said proudly.

Trace forced a smile. 'I hardly remember it myself.' (14)

The elements mix so well that the book was selected the best paperback mystery of the year by the Mystery Writers of America.

The following case, *Too Old a Cat* (Signet, August 1986), has Trace's father, now a NYC private eye, embroiled in a murder case. Trace and Chico journey east to aid him and meet up with two characters from an old series of Murphy's, the screwball police team of Razoni and Jackson. The slam-bang adventures of R & J, begun by Pinnacle in 1973, were brought to an abrupt halt in 1975 after six episodes, probably because they were too close to

other buddy cop series that had become a staple of
books and TV ("Starsky and Hutch" was a watered-
down version, for example).

The ever-prolific Murphy had already completed
a seventh R & J novel and that formed the core of
Cat, with the Trace-related material added. The
result is a mixed bag. The plot, involving sex cultists
and the Mafia, seems all but lost in Murphy's attempt
to provide equal time for five hero-sleuths, two of
whom, Trace and Razoni, seem almost interchangeable.

In March of 1987, the last book in the series,
Getting Up with Fleas, arrived from Signet, marking a
considerable departure from other entries in the
series. The most striking difference is that, after
ninety-plus novels, Murphy finally has written a novel
using the first person narrative. In other Digger and
Trace novels, he includes brief passages in which the
heroes dictate into their frog microphones. Here, the
device, extended to book-length, works marvelously
well, allowing the reader to enter Trace's bizarre mind.
(It should be noted that Trace's narration is not
totally incompatible with the voice the author has used
while writing objectively.)

The yarn begins with Trace having made a
permanent move to New York, "the worst city in the
whole goddamn world except for Bombay," (15) with
Chico remaining in Las Vegas to clean up and close
out their ties there. Both of them have agreed to
work for Tracy and Associates Detective Agency. As
our hero notes: "Sounds impressive, doesn't it? Tracy
and Associates. Until you find out it's a retired cop
(my father), a drunk (me), and a homicidal maniac
(Chico)." (16)

He and the Agency are hired by his old
insurance company bosses to keep tabs on a heavily
insured actor who seems to have become a suicidal

alcoholic immediately after taking out the policy.
Trace is on his own for most of the book. Jackson
and Razoni make a brief guest appearance and depart.
His father, Sarge, has his own case to worry about.
Chico remains in Las Vegas until she is needed to
figure out the denouement.

Much of *Fleas* consists of Trace on his own,
snapping off wisecracks and making offhand
observations:

I think all the time. Just this morning I
was thinking that the people who think Marilyn
Monroe was a tragic figure are generally the
same people who think Robert Blake is a good
actor. And I was thinking that Telly Savalas
isn't the kind of guy you'd trust to watch your
car while you were walking around the corner,
but he's perfect for doing casino commercials
because they're trying to attract people just like
him. (17)

According to Murphy, he decided to end Trace's
career with this novel, because "eleven books of
autobiography are enough for any man." (18) If he
holds to that, he will have ended the saga at its
funniest, highest point.

*

I'm a pretty good problem solver. A
simplifier. Mollie's a complicator. So's Dick. I
always pick smart partners.

--Warren Murphy, in an interview
with the author, July 5, 1984.

Sandwiched in between the series have been a
few mass-market novels, like *The Red Moon* and *The
Ceiling of Hell*, which Murphy labels as "Ludlumesque."

(19)   And there is the most popular of any of his
works, the novel that he wrote with his wife, Molly
Cochran, *Grandmaster* (Pinnacle, Advance Reading
Edition, May 1984).

Cochran's flair for complexity is apparent in this
multilayered tale that introduces a fascinating hero,
Justin Gilead, and an equally fascinating villain,
Alexander Zharkov, chess champions from America and
Russia respectively, equally proficient in international
espionage and Far Eastern mysticism. While the book
is darker and more serious than anything Murphy has
tried, before or since, it is not without his familiar
flashes of humor and sly satire, and includes a
delicious put-down of that pseudonymous fictioneer
Trevanian, whose Shibumi territory *Grandmaster*
successfully invades.

(Justin's) father, a novelist known worldwide
by the single name Leviathan, which graced a
stream of flashy if embarrassingly illiterate best-
sellers . . . (20).

(Murphy, coincidentally, shared credit for the
screenplay based on Trevanian's *The Eiger Sanction*
with Hal Dresner and Rod Whitaker. When asked, in
1978, if he was able to find out the true identity
behind Trevanian's pen name, he replied: "Well, the guy
got credit for writing the movie, and it wasn't Hal
Dresner and it wasn't me. So you figure it out.")

Grandmaster was seven weeks on the *New York
Times* bestseller list and received a 1984 Mystery
Writers of America Award. It was planned as the first
part of a trilogy about Gilead and Zharkov. Book Two,
High Priest, published by New American Library in
November of 1987, continues their adventures as they
battle not only each other but a third enemy, a young
boy with hypnotic powers, who attempts to destroy
them both.

*

Although Murphy seems determined to place all of his new projects between hard covers, he did admit to having "a couple of ideas for Trace that I may get around to. I've also got three finished novels in a drawer somewhere, and two unfinished novels. Along with over fifty outlines.

"And," he concluded with some pride, "I haven't given up on any of 'em." (21)

Notes

(1) Warren Murphy interview, May 5, 1987
(2) Warren Murphy interview, July 5, 1984
(3) Warren Murphy interview, May 5, 1987
(4) *The Assassin's Handbook* (Pinnacle, November 1982, p. 151)
(5) *Ibid.*, p. 159
(6) Warren Murphy interview, January, 1978
(7) *Ibid.*
(8) *Ibid.*
(9) *Ibid.*
(10) Warren Murphy interview, July 5, 1984
(11) Warren Murphy interview, May 5, 1987
(12) Warren Murphy interview, July 5, 1984
(13) *Pigs Get Fat* by Warren Murphy (Signet, October 1985, p. 30)
(14) *Ibid.*, pp. 201-202
(15) *Getting Up with Fleas* by Warren Murphy (Signet, March 1987, p. 10)
(16) *Ibid.*, p. 14
(17) *Ibid.*, p. 10
(18) Warren Murphy interview, May 5, 1987
(19) *Ibid.*
(20) *Grandmaster* by Warren Murphy and Molly Cochran (Pinnacle, Special Advance Reading

Edition, May 1984, p. 51)
(21) Warren Murphy interview, May 5, 1987

Checklist: Warren Murphy

The Arms of Kali (with Richard Sapir) (Signet, 1984)
Assassins Play-Off (with Richard Sapir) (Pinnacle, 1975)
Atlantic City (with Frank Stevens) (Pinnacle, 1979)
Bay City Blast (Pinnacle, 1979)
Blood Ties (with Richard Sapir) (Signet, 1987)
The Bottom Line (with Richard Sapir) (Pinnacle, 1979)
The Ceiling of Hell (Fawcett Crest, 1984)
Chinese Puzzle (with Richard Sapir) (Pinnacle, 1971)
Created, The Destroyer (with Richard Sapir) (Pinnacle, 1971)
Dead Letter (Pocket, 1982)
Death Check (with Richard Sapir) (Pinnacle, 1971)
The Eleventh Hour (with Richard Sapir) (Signet, 1987)
The Final Death (with Richard Sapir) (Pinnacle, 1977)
Fool's Flight (Pocket, 1982)
Fool's Gold (with Richard Sapir) (Pinnacle, 1983)
Funny Money (with Richard Sapir) (Pinnacle, 1975)
Getting Up with Fleas (Signet, 1987)
Grandmaster (with Molly Cochran) (Pinnacle, 1984)
High Priest (with Molly Cochran) (New American Library, 1987) (hardcover)
Kill or Cure (with Richard Sapir) (Pinnacle, 1977)
The Last Temple (with Richard Sapir) (Pinnacle, 1977)
Leonardo's Law (Carlyle, 1978)
Lucifer's Weekend (Pocket, 1982)
Master's Challenge (with Richard Sapir) (Pinnacle, 1984)
Mugger Blood (with Richard Sapir) (Pinnacle, 1977)

Murder's Shield (with Richard Sapir) (Pinnacle, 1973)
Once a Mutt (Signet, 1985)
Pigs Get Fat (Signet, 1985)
Profit Motive (with Richard Sapir) (Pinnacle, 1982)
The Red Moon (Gold Medal, 1982)
Remo: The Adventure Begins (with Richard Sapir)
    (Signet, 1985)
Smoked Out (Pocket, 1982)
Summit Chase (with Richard Sapir) (Pinnacle, 1973)
Sweet Dreams (with Richard Sapir) (Pinnacle, 1976)
Terror Squad (with Richard Sapir) (Pinnacle, 1973)
Too Old a Cat (Signet, 1986)
Total Recall (Pinnacle, 1984)
Trace (Signet, 1983)
Trace and 47 Miles of Rope (Signet, 1984)
Union Bust (with Richard Sapir) (Pinnacle, 1973)
When Elephants Forget (Signet, 1984)

EDITOR'S NOTE: The books are listed above according to the byline(s) that appears on them. In some cases, the actual authorship of the books is different, as seen in the preceding article and in Allen J. Hubin's *Crime Fiction* bibliographies.

ABOUT THE EDITORS AND CONTRIBUTORS

JON L. BREEN, Professor/Librarian at Rio Hondo College in Whittier, California, is the author of four novels, most recently *Touch of the Past* (1988), and a double Edgar winner in the biographical/critical category.

MARTIN HARRY GREENBERG, Professor of Political Science at the University of Wisconsin-Green Bay, is the editor of hundreds of short story anthologies, most of them in the science fiction or mystery fields.

MAX ALLAN COLLINS is author of the Shamus Award-winning *True Detective* (1983), many other novels, and an Edgar-nominated study of Mickey Spillane.

BILL CRIDER, chairman of the English Department at Alvin Community College in Alvin, Texas, is the editor of *Mass Market Publishing in America* (1982) and the author of the Anthony Award-winning *Too Late to Die* (1986).

LOREN D. ESTLEMAN, winner of the Shamus and Spur awards, is one of the leading contemporary novelists in both the mystery and western genres. He is the creator of Detroit private eye Amos Walker.

ED GORMAN, editor and publisher of *Mystery Scene* and founder of the American Crime Writers League, is the author of several novels about private eye Jack Dwyer.

GEORGE KELLEY, Professor of Business
Administration at Erie Community College, Buffalo, New
York, is a contributor to *Twentieth Century Crime and
Mystery Writers* and a frequent reviewer for mystery
fanzines.

MARVIN LACHMAN, perhaps the most prolific
writer for mystery fan periodicals and reference books,
won an Edgar award as one of the editors of
Encyclopedia of Mystery and Detection (1976).

DICK LOCHTE, theatre critic for *Los Angeles*
magazine and frequent book reviewer for the Los
Angeles *Times*, wrote the Edgar-nominated *Sleeping
Dog* (1985).

WILL MURRAY, Editorial Directory of Odyssey
Publications, is a leading authority on pulp magazine
fiction and the author of books on Doc Savage and the
Shadow.

DONALD E. WESTLAKE, who won an Edgar for
God Save the Mark (1967), is one of the most
respected contemporary authors of crime and mystery
fiction. The early volumes in his Parker series (as by
Richard Stark) were paperback originals.

INDEX OF TITLES

INDEX OF NAMES

Miller, Wade, vii
Mitchell, Margaret, 101
Mitford, Nancy, 65
Monroe, Marilyn, 100, 161
Moore, Archie, 22
Moreau, Jeanne, 94
Muller, Marcia, 30
Murphy, Warren, iii, ix, 136, 145, 146, 147, 148, 149, 150, 151, 152, 153, 154, 155, 156, 157, 160, 161, 162, 164
Murray, Will, iii, 135, 154, 155, 168
Myers, Harriet Kathryn, 1
Nixon, Richard, 151
O'Brien, Geoffrey, 90
O'Hara, John, 12, 65
Packer, Vin, iii, ix, 55, 56, 57, 58, 59, 60, 61, 62, 63, 64, 65, 66, 67, 68
Parker, Robert, 157
Patterson, Floyd, 22
Peckinpah, Sam, 36, 47
Pendleton, Donald Eugene, ix, 135, 136, 138, 139, 140, 141, 142, 143, 144, 146
Penzler, Otto, 37
Peterson, Jim, 141, 142
Prather, Richard S., ix, 15
Pronzini, Bill, iii
Quarry, Nick, 76, 78, 87, 88
Queen, Ellery, vii
Quinn, James, 1
Rabe, Peter, iii, ix, 113, 114, 115, 116, 117, 119,

120, 121, 122, 123, 124, 125, 126, 127, 128, 129, 130, 131, 132, 133
Randisi, Robert, 154
Reilly, John, x
Robinson, Sugar Ray, 22
Rohmer, Sax, vii
Rooney, Mickey, 23
Rosenberger, Joseph, 136
Sapir, Richard, 136, 145, 146, 147, 148, 149, 150, 151, 152, 153, 154, 164, 165
Savalas, Telly, 161
Shibuk, Charles, iii
Sinatra, Frank, 79
Smith, Thorne, 116
Spielberg, Stephen, 95
Spillane, Mickey, vii, 15, 38, 138
Stark, Richard, 168
Stevens, Frank, 164
Stout, Rex, 156
Stuart, Clay, 1
Tavernier, Bertrand, 36
Thompson, Jim, iii, viii, 13, 35, 36, 37, 38, 39, 40, 41, 42, 43, 44, 45, 46, 47, 48, 49, 50, 51, 52, 53, 54, 128
Trevanian, 162
Twain, Mark, 42
Tyson, Nona, 95
Von Elner, Don, ix, x
Ward, Fred, 149
Welles, Orson, 93, 94
Westlake, Donald E., iii, 113, 148, 168
Whitaker, Rod, 162
White, Harry, 1